Bittersweet Legacy

To Ben, a survivor and friend, love Barbara

Creative Responses to the Holocaust

Art   Poetry   Stories

Edited by
CYNTHIA MOSKOWITZ BRODY

Foreword by Michael Berenbaum

Studies in the Shoah

Volume XXIV

University Press of America, Inc.
Lanham • New York • Oxford

Copyright © 2001 by
University Press of America,® Inc.
4720 Boston Way
Lanham, Maryland 20706

12 Hid's Copse Rd.
Cumnor Hill, Oxford OX2 9JJ

Library of Congress Cataloging-in-Publication Data

Bittersweet legacy : creative responses to the Holocaust : art,
poetry, stories / edited by Cynthia Moskowitz Brody ;
foreword by Michael Berenbaum.
p. cm
1. Holocaust, Jewish (1939-1945)—Influence. 2. Holocaust,
Jewish (1939-1945)—Literary collections. 3. Holocaust, Jewish
(1939-1945), in art. I. Brody, Cynthia Moskowitz.
D804.3 .B556 2001 940.53'18—dc21 2001017130 CIP

ISBN 0-7618-1975-4 (cloth : alk. paper)
ISBN 0-7618-1976-2 (pbk. : alk. paper)

To My Parents,
Ernest Moskowitz and Hermina Hauer Moskowitz
who survived the Holocaust
as they each enter their 80th year.
And
to their parents, Samuel and Pepi Hauer and
Chaim and Sarah Klein Moskowitz,
their sisters and brothers, Morris and Alexander Moskowitz,
Zsenny and Serena Hauer
and the children, Manci, Mayshu, Zoly, Andy, Laychy and the baby
all taken too soon.

This book is a memorial to you and to
all of the families we never knew.
We are honored to carry your names
and continue to create in your memory.

Contributing Artists

Marcia Annenberg
Cynthia Moskowitz Brody
Harley Gaber
Chandra Garsson
Chaim Goldberg
Judy Herzl
Wolf Kahn
Sherry Karver
Toan Klein
Lisa Kokin
Leah Korican
Harold Lewis
Barbara Milman
Rosa Naparstek
Lauren Herzog Schwartz
Sharon Siskin
Barbara Leventhal-Stern
Elly Simmons
Denise Satter
Dorrit Title
Deborah Trilling
Irv Wieder

Contributing Authors

Yehuda Amichai
Sari Aviv
Chana Bloch
Cynthia Moskowitz Brody
Ruth Daigon
Enid Dame
Cortney Davis
Annie Dawid
Adam Fisher
Charles Fishman
Jacqueline Fishman
Harry Fiss
Stewart Florsheim
Paula Naomi Friedman
David Gershator
Beth Aviv Greenbaum
Lizlotte Erlanger Glozer
Eva Gross
Annette Bialik Harchik
Roald Hoffmann
Irena Klepfisz
Yala Korwin
Gabriel Ariel Levicky
Lyn Lifshin
Leatrice Lifshitz
Joan Lipkin
Cecile Low

Janet Marks
Ruth Marmorstein
Seymour Mayne
Odette Meyers
Rochelle Natt
Gary Pacernick
Heidemarie Pilc
Evelyn Posamentier
Dahlia Ravikovich
Liliane Richman
Shula Robin
Elizabeth Rosner
Bonnie Salomon
Vera Schwartz
Myra Sklarew
Elizabeth Anne Socolow
Jason Sommer
Hans Jorg Stahlschmidt
Elaine Starkman
Hannah Stein
Susan Terris
Barbara Unger
Henny Wenkart
Ruth Whitman
Juliet Zarembsky
Laura Zusman

Contents

Foreword

Theodore Adorno commented that writing poetry after Auschwitz is barbaric. Martin Buber has written:

> The more powerful the response, the more powerfully it ties down the You and as by a spell binds it into an object. Only silence toward the You, the silence of all tongues, the taciturn waiting in the unformed, undifferentiated pre-linguistic word leaves the You free and stands together with it in reserve where the spirit does not manifest itself but is. *All response binds the You into the It world. That is the melancholy of man, and also that is his greatness.* For thus knowledge, thus works, thus image and example come into being among the living. (*I and Thou*, pp. 89-89 Walter Kaufmann translation, italics mine).

Irving Howe, the distinguished literary critic asked: "Is the debris of our misery (as one survivor described it) a proper or manageable subject for stories and novels? Are there not perhaps extreme situations beyond the reach of art?" The questions that are asked of one imaginative art form also apply to the others whether they be art or literature, poetry, sculpture or music.

And yet there can be no doubt that poetry has been written, good poetry, powerful poetry that seeks to come to terms with the destruction of European Jewry. Poetry has been written even in the German language in powerful works by Nelly Sachs and Paul Celan for example.

And yet there also can be no doubt that the silence has been broken, even by those such as Elie Wiesel who long for silence, who argue for silence, who plead for silence.

Still, there also can also be no doubt that despite the acknow-ledgement that there are extreme situations beyond the reach of art, the artist must confront that limit, must move toward the abyss and must create from it.

It is with these thoughts in mind that one reads this collection of poetry, stories and art that Cynthia Brody had edited with such care and dedication. The authors, the artists, are diverse—Jews and non-Jews; those linked directly to the Event as witnesses, survivor artists; those linked by bonds of kinship, the second generation and the third; those who inherited the Holocaust as an atrocity that happened to their people, the Jewish people, and those who inherited it as some-thing that happened to their people, the human family. They wrestle to understand and to express, to give voice and form to what has be-come a defining, signature event of 20th century humanity. With all due respect to the reservations of grappling with the Holocaust, could we also not ask: how can one not give voice to this moment in history which robs art of a simplicity of understanding, which demands that forms be pushed to their limits to express the inexpressible, to appre-hend the ineffable?

I must confess that I am somewhat troubled by the title. I under-stand that the Holocaust has become our Bitter Legacy. I write these words in South Africa after a week of meetings with those who struggled against apartheid and those who struggle against the bitter residue of apartheid. It is a time of hope in South Africa, a time to overcome the residue of oppression. Even here, among these men, the Holocaust is a legacy of the century past, respected for what it shares in common with the racism of apartheid and for where racism was taken to its most extreme forms, systematic state-sponsored murder undertaken by the state in institutions created to facilitate total annihilation. So the Bitter Legacy is understood, the bittersweet is not.

But like my colleague Lawrence Langer, I believe that the ulti-mate truth of the Holocaust is found in the darkness, that authentic creation must confront that darkness and not back away from it by seeking easy grace in the moments of decency and humanity that from time to time offered a ray of light.

In this anthology diverse authors of greater and lesser talents are represented, but their efforts make use of their talents, require the best of their talents. The results are impressive, the shattering insights of-fered by poetry are joined with the powerful emotions conveyed by art and enhanced by the fragments of memory and legacy transmitted in story. Because of the variety of authors and the diversity of points of view, *Bittersweet Legacy* is a document of its time, it conveys with authority the way in which the Holocaust is perceived in our time.

Fifty five years from today when a generation more than a century away from the Holocaust and almost a generation removed from the last of the survivors asks, how did that generation—the only generation—to live at a distance from the Shoah and yet still in the presence of its eyewitnesses respond to that Event and give voice to it, they would not be unwise to turn to this anthology for it is a collective expression of its time.

Michael Berenbaum
Los Angeles, California
Johannesburg, South Africa
November 2000

Michael Berenbaum is a writer, lecturer, and teacher consulting in the conceptual development of museums and the historical development of films. He is also an adjunct Professor of Theology at the University of Judaism in Los Angeles. For three years, he was President and Chief Executive Officer of the Survivors of the Shoah Visual History Foundation. Prior to that he was the Director of the United States Holocaust Research Institute and Project Director of the Museum During Its Creation. Berenbaum is the author and editor of twelve books, scores of scholarly articles. Among his books are *The World Must Know* and *The Bombing of Auschwitz: Should the Allies Have Attempted It?*

Preface

When I was small I knew very little, but I knew one thing that many others did not know. I knew that something had happened that was so terrible that no one would speak about it. I sensed that other children knew nothing about this, and I had no desire to be the one to reveal the information. The Holocaust had happened to my family and to me. It was our dark secret. My mother had been in a place called Auschwitz . . . somewhere far away where she had to sleep on wooden bunks and wondered what she had done that was so bad that she could not even have a pillow. My father had been a prisoner on forced labor. Both of them had been through too much, had lost all that was important to them. There was a haunted look about them. When, at age five, I asked my parents why I did not have any grandparents I was told "because the Germans killed them. When I asked for the reason my mother told me "because they were Jewish" as if this were explanation enough. The rest was left up to my imagination, but the seed had been planted for unbounded fear that my family was in danger, the world was a treacherous place and that human beings had within them the capacity for real evil. This haunted me for most of my childhood. As more information came to the surface I began to realize that my parents had outwitted death, by some unexplainable twist of fate, and so I had been allowed a life. The feeling of responsibility that accompanied such a realization was substantial. If, statistically speaking, I should never have been born, I felt I must be here to do something very important. No matter what I did, it never seemed enough for the price that had been paid. Additionally, the "memories" that I had inherited hung like a weight around my neck and there seemed no way to relieve myself of the burden. I could not talk to my parents about the Holocaust because I knew this would be painful for them to remember and I did not want to further burden them with worry. Although the message of evil had been passed on to me at a very early age, I was still expected to be happy. Expressions of fear or sadness—emotions they were desperately trying to repress in themselves, were not tolerated well. This double message in addition to natural feelings of protectiveness towards my parents led me to keep my true feelings, fears and questions to myself. My friends seemed oblivious to the Holocaust even though most of them were Jewish. I was on my own in trying to live quietly while this internal monster devoured me.

Upon entering adolescence, I discovered in myself a newly budding artistic talent. I had finally found something I was good at and began spending most of my time drawing, often when I should have been taking notes in school. As the years passed I began painting and developing my own style, one which combined beauty with wistfulness, always feeling I could not portray life as carefree or only focus on the beauty, as that would be ignoring the darkness which still exists amidst the beauty. I felt the need to express something of importance about the Holocaust, but was terrified to even begin an effort. I was afraid that once I began, I would be swallowed up in the horrifying imagery. It took forty years to take that risk. What I discovered was often to the contrary. In allowing the darkness into the light of day I gained control over it. I could select the imagery and wipe it away in one swipe of the rag. When I chose to use words as my medium, I could finally say out loud what no one cared to hear before, and I felt better once the laboring words were delivered. As the pieces became more personal in recent years, they were often accompanied by tears and nightmares. Still, the poison had begun to make its way out of my mind and my body, and in so doing had transformed into a thing of beauty. The very cause of the suffering was the inspiration for creativity, a lasting attempt at understanding a reality that was unfathomable.

This same feeling has been repeated a hundred fold in the experience of gathering materials for this anthology. I was drawn to the San Francisco area in June of 1994 knowing no one but my daughter, Julie, who was attending graduate school. Within a few months of arriving I found myself in an intergenerational group for Holocaust survivors and children of survivors. This was my first experience of sharing my past with anyone who would listen. I also listened. What I heard were references to poetry, stories, and music and art that these people had created in response to their experiences. What struck me with great force was the fact that, like me, others had used creative means to try to integrate their painful experiences about the Holocaust, and much of that material might never be seen because of its private nature. I knew in that moment that I had to bring those creative expressions out into the world. I sensed that they would be extremely powerful and would lend greater understanding of how the Holocaust affected those who survived it as well as those who inherited its legacy. What I did not expect was the far-reaching impact on people of many varied backgrounds. Another discovery was that the subject of the Holocaust continues to burn into the human conscience and consciousness and as a result new images continue to be forged even now, over fifty years since its end. There seems to be a continuous epilogue to the story of the Holocaust.

Included in this anthology are many different Holocaust experiences. Some come from American Jews who lost no family members, yet were changed permanently as human beings upon learning of its horrors. They too needed a place to express their feelings, and I believe they belong here, alongside the works of those who have experiential memories. The work of survivors, their children and grandchildren are replete with intense imagery and emotion and it is clear that the trauma was transmitted through the generations. What was also passed on was a sense of survival. Although the stories, images and themes reflect the pain of this darkest time in history, those who created them have used their own power of artistic thought, drive and determination, to look the monster in the face and transform it into something that can finally be seen, if not understood.

My regret is that the richness and variety of color present in much of the art cannot be appreciated because of the limitations of black and white printing. Color offers the element of hope and celebration of life that the imagery may not convey in its present form. Still, the imagery and symbolism are of great significance. This relates to my reasons for selecting *Bittersweet Legacy-Creative Responses to the Holocaust* as the title for this collection. I am aware that this event, the Holocaust, was filled with bitterness and horror, the aftereffects of which we as a human race continue to experience. My belief is that the continuation of the faith, the clinging to important, ancient values is a sweetness that lives as well in this legacy. As an artist I have experienced both the bitterness and sweetness in the creation of images relating to this experience. I see the creative process as a gift with which we can begin to exorcise the pain. I have always seen life after the Holocaust as a vital merging of the most awful with the most beautiful, life where there was and would have been only death. Finally, the sweetness of hope, which allows us to continue living after all of the loss.

Those of us who, as individuals, were creating in a vacuum, unheard and unseen, are now being given the opportunity to give voice to the millions whose voices were silenced. They too were only individuals, seemingly unimportant as such, but overwhelming in the company of six million others like themselves. Those artists and writers who have had the courage to create from their own darkness come together in this book to forge their collective voices into a song of truth that can finally be shared.

Cynthia Moskowitz Brody

Acknowledgments

Many thanks to the Judah Magnes Museum for suggesting award-winning poets for *Bittersweet Legacy* and for establishing a fund in its name. I would also like to thank Michael Berenbaum for being the first to recognize the value of this project and for his support in its publication. My gratitude to Zev Garber for including this collection in the Shoah Series. I am also appreciative of the quotes provided by Stephen Feinstein. I am grateful to my good friend, Robert Zadek, whose generosity helped to make the dream a reality. Many thanks to the artists and writers of *Bittersweet Legacy* for contributions, artistic and financial, and for the many notes of encouragement throughout the years since the inception of this project.

I appreciate the support of Lisa Kay and Cheryl Levine for entry of data early on, Dorothy Albritton for final preparation and reminding me to breathe, and Donald White for his careful proofing. Thank you to Jay Daniel of Black Cat Sudio for his scanning and preparation of all photographs for reproduction. Finally, a thank you to my family and friends for quietly listening as I fretted over this project for over six years, and for believing in me.

**Co-published by The Judah Magnes Museum,
Berkeley, California.**

Acknowledgments for Copyright Permission

Irena Klepfisz- "The Widow and Daughter" Reprinted from *A Few Words in the Mother Tongue: Poems Selected and New by* Irena Klepfisz (1990) Reprinted with the kind permission of the author and Eight Mountain Press.

Seymour Mayne- "If when you hear me":from *The Impossible Promised Land: Poems New and Selected* (Mosaic Press/Valley Editions, 1981), copyright ©Seymour Mayne, 1981, 2000. All rights reserved by the author

Barbara Milman- "Auschwitz #10" and "Auschwitz #6" previously published in *Light in the Shadows* by Barbara Milman (Jonathan David Publishers, Inc)

Barbara Reisner- "Warsaw, 1946", "A Little Beethoven in the Background", "A Scene from the Deportation" previously published in *Poets On*: "Until the Day Breathe" previously published in *Creeping Bent* and *The Laurel Review*

Jackie Fishman- "Café Mit Schlag" first published in *Jewish Bulletin of Northern California*

Joan Lipkin- Story "Silent Night" previously published in *Nice Jewish Girls: Growing Up in America*, edited by Marlene Adler Marks in 1996, Plume/Penguin Books

Jason Sommer- "Meyer Tsits and the Children", "Joining the Story" previously published in *Lifting the Stone* (Forest Books, London)

Evelyn Posamentier- "The Bird Named Isidore" and "Counting Backwards" were both previously published in *Ghosts of the Holocaust*, (Wayne State Univ., 1989) by permission. "Counting Backwards" appeared in *The American Poetry Review* (Feb/Mar 1978)

Hans Stahlschmidt- "If you could lick my heart", "Germans and Jews", "The German Language", The Limits of Language", first published in *Wetlands* (Small Poetry Press, 1998).

Ruth Whitman- Excerpts from *The Testing of Hannah Senesh* (Wayne State University Press, 1986)

Lilian Richman- "After Claude Lanzman, Shoah 1987" first published *in Blood to Remember* by Barbara Unger (Texas Tech University Press, 1991). "The Refugee", previously published in *The Literary Review*. "Sparing the Children" and "A Jewish Education" first published in *Blue Depression Glass* by Barbara Unger (Thorntree Press)

Chana Bloch- "Mother Hunger" from *Mrs. Dumpty* by Chana Bloch (Madison: Univerity of WisconsinPress, 1998) "Abuse"from *The Window:Nnew and Selected Poems* by Dahlia Ravikovitch, translated by Chana Bloch and Ariel Bloch (New York: The Sheep Meadow Press, 1989)

"Almost a Love Poem"- from *The Selected Poetry of Yehuda Amichai*, translated by Chana Bloch and Stephen Mitchell (Berkeley: University of California Press, 1996)

Lislotte Erlanger Gloser- Previously published in *Reconstructionist, 1987*

Elizabeth Rosner-owns rights- "Ghosts" previously published in: *A Quarterly Journal of Jewish Life and Thought* published by the American Jewish Congress, NY, NY.

Eliabeth Anne Socolow- "Going In: Images of the Holocaust" previously published in *Wayzgoose*, 1991

Jason Sommer- "Joining the Story" and "Meyer Tsits and the Children" and "The Breaking of the Glass" in slightly different form published in *Lifting the Stone*.

"Joining the Story" and "Meyer Tsits and the Children" appeared also in *Other People's Troubles* in their current versions.

Odette Meyers- "Dreams of a Nunnery" passage from Doors to Madame Marie, pp 329-334 excerpted from *Doors to Madame* Reprinted by permission of the University of Washington Press, 1997

Gary Pacernick- "Warsaw 1937" first published in *JEWISH CURRENTS* 41, no. 1 (445), January, 1987.

Ruth Daigon- from *Moon Inside* by Ruth Daigon..

Leatrice Lifshitz- "Lost Faces" appeared in *A Poem in a Pamphlet*

Enid Dame- "Soup" was published in *Anything You Don't See* by West End Press, 1992 .

Charles Fishman- "The Young Germans" previously published in *European Judaism*
"The Youngest Known Holocaust Survivor" *first published in The Genocide Forum*
"The Survivors are Dying" first published in *Medicinal Purposes*
"Not Only in the Six Day War" first published in *Ghosts of the Holocaust*
"How to Read Holocaust Poems" first published in *The Death Mazurka*

Myra Sklarew- "Becoming a Jew"- first published in *Altamira*, 1987
"April 1943 Borszczow"- previously published in *Lithuania: New and Selected Poems* 1995,1997
"On Muranowska St"owns rights, previously published in *Lithuania: New and Selected Poems,* 1995, 1997
"Blessed Art Thou No-One"- previously published in *The Science of Goodbyes*

Roald Hoffman- "Natural History" and " Speaker for the Dead" previously published in *Chelsea* and *Midstream*, respectively.

Susan Terris- "Hidden Child", *Tikkun* Dreaming Theresienstadt, *Poets On*, "To My Children"appeared in *The Jewish Spectator*, but the rights are hers. This poem, in its present form, has appeared in her chapbook, *EYE OF THE HOLOCAUST* (Arctos Press, 1999)

Elaine Starkman- "In the Kibbutz Laundry" published by Judah Magnes in *Without A Single Answer: Poems of Contemporary Israel* and *Coming Together*, Sheer Press

Cortney Davis- "Conversion was first published in *Sifrut*(Jewish Bulletin of N Ca), winter 1992, winner of Rosenberg award for Judah Magnes Museum.

Shula Robin- "German Tourist's Daughter" first published in I *Know Who I Am* by Shula Robin

Henny Wenkart- First Swastika Season initially published in *SARAH'S DAUGHTERS SING* (KTAV 1990)

Eva Gross- "The Last Jewish Woman in Mor", first printed in *JUF NEWS* of Chicago.

Barbara Unger- "Tantrums" first published in *Crazyquilt*, vol. 5, No. 1 March 1990.
"Sparing the Children" first published in *Blue Depression Glass* by Barbara Unger

Yala Korwin- "I Dreamed Him Homeward" first published in *Midstream*

Sharon Siskin- "Invisible" first published in *Davka* Magazine

Hannah Stein- "Twin" first published in *The American Voice*.

Annie Dawid- "Listening to Deutschland: 1980" first published in Winter, 1990 No. 57 *Response: a Contemporary Jewish Review*

Chapter Introductions

1. The American Experience of the Holocaust

The first chapter deals with the way in which information about the Holocaust slipped into American Jewish households and how parents tried to shield their children from the horrors. It also reveals the level at which denial operated in this country in regard to the extremity of the situation overseas and the connection to anti-Semitism being experienced by those who lived here. The experiences of survivors of the Holocaust have been presented in autobiographies, films and oral histories. Because of the intensity of those stories, many people who were not personally involved felt it was not appropriate to make their own pain and fear public. Those who write of their experiences in America were just children at the time of World War II. They had little understanding of the secrecy adopted by their families and society as a whole. Now, looking back on this mysterious time, they express resentment at being protected from the truth. We have to wonder how that truth would have affected them and whether their parents unknowingly allowed them a short time when they could sustain innocence and just be children. They could have a period free from the burdens that would be carried once the horrors were exposed and embodied. Many people remember the first time they were exposed to the atrocities of the Holocaust in the form of school or movie theater documentaries. Often it created a state of dissociation, so unbelievable were the visions. Families still struggle with deciding when to impart this dark history and parents often put off the task until the children are old enough to comprehend that kind of darkness and suffering. Still, it is inevitable that the innocence of childhood will be altered upon receipt of this information. As difficult as it is in the present, the combination of fear and even a desire to distance from the Jewish identity for safety purposes, may have played a part in the secretive nature of the American experience of the Holocaust. Several of the artists represented, although they lost no immediate family members, were so affected by the atrocities that they have found themselves creating entire series on the subject of the Holocaust. Interestingly, these artists seem able to utilize more explicit visual symbolism than some of the children of survivors. Perhaps the emotional distance earlier in life allowed the deep exploration through art which some children of survivors may feel to be psychologically threatening. These Americans present to us their own undeniable products of pain and empathy in an attempt to be heard and to foster change in the world we live in today.

II. Through the Eyes of a Child

Chapter two allows us to see with a clear child's vision the depth of emotion experienced as the Holocaust progressed in Eastern Europe. Poems and stories reflect on the bizarre fashion in which children were removed from their families, raised by others, sometimes in another faith, and then returned years later to the families they no longer remembered. It questions the definition of family and brings to light the confusion and rootlessness that became the foundation set for these children. And yet, they have grown up to be insightful, sensitive adults. Some practice Christianity and Judaism in an attempt to stay loyal to both faiths that formed their identity. All who have contributed to this collection have shown the resilience that children can embody. Some create from their memories of a life in hiding, when freedom of speech and hunger took on new meaning. Stories unfold about systematic losses and the parents' desire to provide safe havens for their children. And most unfathomable, memories of life as a child in a concentration camp, where often the focus is on concerns for siblings, parents, and the basic bodily needs which were no longer provided for. There exists an attitude of innocence combined with a dark wisdom about the truth. These children became aware of the evil that many people today still do not comprehend. They rose from a childhood steeped in ashes to deliver their memories, their hopes and their visions to us.

III. Survival

In this, perhaps the most chilling and poignant of all the chapters, stories and images come forth which attempt to portray a truth that humanity can barely comprehend. There are not words or symbols enough to adequately portray the Holocaust experience. For many years the whole subject was avoided in art, sometimes even considered inappropriate or disrespectful. In that period of time there are those who have chosen to revise Holocaust history, deny its depth and breadth. These representations of individual experiences draw the reader into a private world, one that is believable. These works were selected because they touch the heart and open it to receive what might otherwise be overwhelming. Each poem is like a photograph, taking in as many images of the environment, the internal state and in some cases the visceral bodily feelings of the subject. The repeated symbols of railroad tracks, bones, weary feet, emaciation and even clothing devoid of people who had worn them resonate with the written imagery. Themes surface which honor the bravery, loyalty and even hope of those who did not know if they would survive. Values are passed from father to son, friend to friend, in a desperate attempt to leave something of importance behind. The visual symbolism is very strong; utilizing irony such as concentration camp shirts made of hog's gut. A torah scroll lies in the grips of a vise decorated with a swastika. The swastika appears in many forms; paintings, sculptures and mixed media designs, its insidious message loud and clear. Stories also form around the continuation of the haunting as survivors carry their memories into their new lives after the war.

IV. Inheritance

The title reflects the effects of the Holocaust on the families of those who lived through this experience. There is a resounding cry from children of survivors who have carried their own fears, confusion and anger about their past. Some felt the need to protect their parents from anything negative, thus finding themselves isolated with their terror and sadness. Some speak of wanting to learn more about the secrets while also fearing what details might prove too difficult to bear. With each new bit of information came a permanent, inextricable vision created in horrific imagery. Without the details, parents and other ancestors remained cut off from these children. Some reveal their own frightful imagination, seemingly inherited through stories or unexplained questions. The Holocaust represented suffering on such a grand scale that often children of survivors did not feel their problems compared with the life and death travails their parents had endured. They mourn never having had grandparents or other extended family and the images of ghosts make many appearances in the art and writing. All seem to feel the need to impart this information that was often kept secret for so long. Several describe returning to the site of the horrors and the incredulity of a world that goes on where their parents' world was destroyed. Adolescent poets display the transmission of the experience through the generations with words and thoughts far beyond their years. It is clear from the creative works in this chapter that the Holocaust did not end with D day. Its effects continue to unfold in the families of those who live in its shadow.

V. Facing the Enemy

Much has been written recently about the mentality of those who went along with the precepts of the Holocaust. For many years movies revolved around themes of WWII where the American soldiers won the war. Not much was mentioned about the feelings of the victims toward their persecutors. Perhaps the pain was too deep in those who were trying to establish new lives and not draw attention to themselves. A generation later, questions are still being asked about the enemy. There seems to be a desire to understand motivation, and some poems were born of programs where children of Germans and children of survivors spend a weekend together to work through these intense feelings. Several of the poems that are included express the desire to understand, to connect, and struggle with whether or not forgiveness is appropriate. Included is the perspective of a German son who also struggles with incredible sadness combined with the eternal questions of his own family and nation. Visual imagery includes the machinery of the Holocaust constructed in sculptural form. Poetry dips into past and present images of Germany as German Jews return for visits and must reconcile themselves to the land of their ancestry, the land that also determined to end that lineage forever. In these pieces there are melancholy memories of a time when family was united, when culture and study were a part of everyday life. Intermingled are reminders, like blades cutting through old photographs, of systematically being denied that life until life itself became denied. There is sadness and anger and also a desire to understand and put these long unresolved feelings to rest. There is a need to believe that this will not recur, that people are still people and not monsters.

VI. Chosen

The term "the Chosen People" has been an emotionally loaded one for centuries. This chapter looks at what it is to be chosen, in the biblical sense as well as chosen to be annihilated. There are questions of God in the face of the Holocaust. Did God see? If so, what does that imply about the continuation of faith and the practice of Judaism? For many, the Holocaust experience taught them what was truly meaningful to their lives. Poems speak of creating music in the death camps, of the value of friendship and sharing of meager provisions. Survivors tell us to remember people as individuals—for who they were before they died so brutally. Defining oneself as a Jew after the Holocaust is questioned. Secular Jews look at the ancient sects that continue in their practices as they did for centuries and wonder at their commitment and faith. And finally, the concept of heroism is explored. Heroes thrived in the form of the righteous who hid Jews at their own risk. Mothers died to protect their children. Prisoners who were near death themselves cared for others and expressed their humanity. All who lived through this great darkness proved themselves to be heroic in their efforts to survive and to pass on the faith and traditions of Judaism.

I.

The American Experience of the Holocaust

from SPARING THE CHILDREN

Barbara Unger

Our parents edited war news
so it wouldn't disturb our dreams
or perfect report cards
or cast a rancid smell
over our home life, hanging
like a damp overcoat
in the hall closet

A JEWISH EDUCATION
Barbara Unger

I learn in America
there are two kinds:

Ruthie's the swarthy kind.
Little can be expected
from a refugee's daughter,
a greenhorn.

I'm the good kind,
a Jewish blonde
chewing her braids
as Milton Cross ponders
and the Saturday opera plays.

Shiksa nose like Mother,
ice-blue eyes like God's.

Spaldings crackle against
stoop and curb, *Roosevelt,*
Hitler. On sandy Iwo Jima,
marines stake a windswept flag.

The tears of the Holocaust
banish my Christmas stars and
sugar angel to the closet's
topmost shelf.

In Van Cortlandt Park
a boy spits *dirty Jew*
before the rock he throws
grazes my eye.

Mother's mouth clamps shut
and opens only to announce
dinner or early bed.
She cannot be blamed.

Father reads in the club chair,
refuses to see
my toothcomb stitches
above the eye.
Even a blue eye heals slowly.

In Warsaw they have started
to arm the Ghetto
hide the children.

Figure 1.1   Barbara Leventhal-Stern   "The Roots of Pain Go Deep"

Figure 1.2   Sharon Siskin   "Invisible"

CONVERSION
Cortney Davis

In class I repeat words
that sound like poetry—
tefilah, tsedakah, Torah.
Hebrew letters inch across the page
like iron filings teased by a magnet,
foreign sounds I try to capture

in my throat. Friday nights
I stutter prayers, light
white candles that hiss
at such an awkward blessing.
The rabbi discouraged me,
three times said the words *oppressed*

and *banished*. Three times I said
I understood. Then at work my boss
takes a dollar from his pocket,
raises it like a prize out of reach.
Doubles it, rubs it against itself
as if to spark a flame.

He smiles. *Huh?*
He says, *huh?* And secretive,
as if we shared a joke, whispers
Have you turned Jew enough to jump for it?
I have no words.
He doesn't know if I owned the world

I would give the world away.
The dollar flickers. He tosses it.
My face glows red, catches fire.
Clothes smoke, then flare.
The air stinks of burning bone.
The innocent dollar disappears.

Smoldering, cold, I have received
my first real lesson.

from GOING IN: IMAGES OF THE HOLOCAUST AS I KNEW IT, A JEWISH CHILD IN AMERICA

I.NEIGHBORHOODS
i.Then and now
Elizabeth Anne Socolow

When I was small in Germantown,
                where my grandfather
                        of the flatiron obsession took me walking,
        to Karl Schurz Park
                where the horseshoe of steps
welcomed a skipping girl to dare to walk along its edge,
        and rollerskate along the shallow stairs,
                where my Welsh nanny took me to Mass
        daily at St Joseph's church,
                with the red sandstone facade
                        like the color of Freiburg's Munster,
        when the schwastikas appeared on the *Bierstube* doors
                and the German songs came out the windows,
        where we had Christmas for Agnes and Hannukah
        for all of us, where the deaf mute tailors lived upstairs
and joined us in the basement in the deep Schwarzewald
        of black shades for airraids with their forest green facings,
                where, winter mornings I went to that basement
and watched the bigger brother, John, stoke the coal furnace,
        we had a German butcher. It was not a joke, and he was witty.
        I am the German Butcher, he would say, more sadly
than any sadness in this new world, I do remember his name.
                It had field in it, and brook.
And I want him to save this world as he saved my world at four.

        Each week we went for me, to buy the hard,
                round red tokens, a lamb chop.
                        And once, solemn as a Priest, or Rabbi at Mass

        or Atonement,
raining out, the background noise of rain,
        my red boots on the black and white tile floor,

sawdust scattered, I still can see, the wood against the tile,
　　　　the tan against the black and white, and my red boots,
an image
　　　without figure
　　　　　spelling hope,
　　　forever after, the beehive of those old
hexagons in old shops, black and white,
　　　　　he stepped.
And handed me a brown paper bag, not the color of sawdust,
My child's eye keen on that small difference, paper, not wood,
　　　　　　and pointed at the floor, and handed me the bag.
　　　His blue eyes held the rain in them behind his glasses, and
　　　　　he let them shine not drop
　　　　　　　somehow, not drop.

I put that sawdust down to save the people, so they will not slip,
or fall. It makes a mess. I sweep it up each night, before I close
the shop. I do that for the people, do you see, because I care.
And save your lambchop because I care that you grow strong.
We're not all—All Germans are not—even Butchers are not—
butchers who hate the sawdust mess so much they let the people
slip and fall, and break.

How can one fail to hope that side will win forever in all the world
with such a memory?

The smell in Germany is of plants that look as still as wood,
　　　　　cactus in a sandy mesa.
Nowhere gas. Nowhere the pungency
　　　　of burned bones.
　　　　　　　But in the curved backs of winter vines along the
Rhine, the millions of tended branches not yet pendant with leaf or grape,
　　　　　I still see the twisted bodies of the vanished

How can I trust with such a memory?
　　　How can I judge without it?
　　　　　How can I choose hope?

I watch the news, like you.

In dark hours what still assaults me
like a dream of a whole life slipping
past the sight of a dying soul:
We're not all—Germans are not all—butchers—are not butchers—

RED BOOTS
    IN CLUMPS OF SAWDUST
        AGAINST POLISHED TILES,
        BLACK
            AND
                WHITE.

THE JEWISH EXPERIENCE
Vera Schwartz

On the tour bus
we were all so impatient.
The overindulgent mama and papa,
she with her bandy short legs,
he wizened, his face a mask of dyspepsia,
the numbers, blue on their pallid arms.
Their little American daughter,
worn like an emblem,
whiny, demanding, loud.
"Somebody shut her up!" we took turns
hissing, behind clenched jaws.
At Yad Vashem, they fell
helpless, sobbing, on their knees,
clutched in a desperate embrace.
Their little American daughter,
terrified,
forced her bony arms between them.
"Mama, Papa, get up…get up…
take care of me…"
We looked away, and were silent.

Figure 1.3   Barbara Leventhal-Stern   "You Can't Drown it Out"

TANTRUMS
Barbara Unger

The Holocaust was a well-kept secret back on the broad boulevards of the Northern Bronx in the Forties, especially in those creamy Art Deco buildings along Mosholu Parkway where assimilated Jews like my parents chose to live. I'd heard vague stories of labor camps, but not until Chava's arrival did the true destiny of my European cousins, uncles and aunts become clear to me.

A vivacious Polish refugee half Grandpa's age, Chava was his second wife. With her curly black halo of curls and broad rosy face, she quickly took the place of my dead Grandma Rose. Chava went about fixing up the old house. Once again, golden knadlech floated in chicken soup, and kugel and beef bubbled in the oven. It was heaven to smell the aromas that wafted from Chava's kitchen. My presence there never seemed to bother her.

One by one, Chava conquered the skeptical relatives. She even gained the approval of the ancient family matriarch, Great Aunt Bella Ginsberg. My mother remained the only holdout. Under her breath, my mother muttered that Chava was nothing but an ignorant greenhorn who cared only for Grandpa's money. The requisite year of mourning for Grandma Rose had not elapsed before this youthful interloper was installed in her place. In an incautious moment my mother expressed her conviction that Grandpa and Chava had been "carrying on" while Grandma Rose lay dying.

"Don't worry," said my mother in a voice like that of the prophets. "She's after something. Time will tell. It will all come out in the end."

On Sundays when we visited Grandpa's house in Queens, I derived a ghoulish pleasure in peering at the unlucky bed in which Grandma Rose's leaking and ailing body had lain for a year. Now a neat peach chenille spread covered the crescent.

Eager to trick Chava into confessing her sins, I asked how she and Grandpa met. Without turning a hair, she replied, "On the Lower East Side. Somebody introduced us."

"Was Grandma Rose alive then?" I asked

"A wonderful woman, your grandmother. What could I do? I had a child to support."

This inadvertent admission upset me. At once I felt guilty for tricking this confession from her. In our family, the way to absolve blunders was to make a story out of the blunder. Thus, Chava launched into the tale of how she and her daughter, Lily, had escaped from Hitler. Lost in the spell of her storytelling, I forgot Grandma Rose. Who could compare to this dark-eyed vamp who had not only captured my grandfather's heart but who had also managed to outwit the Arch-fiend Hitler himself?

As she scraped the bowl, Chava spoke in sudden outbursts. "Believe me, we were the lucky ones. It was a miracle to get out alive. The rest of my family was left behind to perish." The story of how she and Lilly had spent the years of the war crouching in a dark damp basement filled me with awe. All I knew of Lilly was that she was a girl about my own age and lived with friends on the Lower East Side. I'd seen her only once on a Sunday visit and recalled only a trace of an accent in her speech and her permed honey-colored hair a shade darker than mine.

"How come Lilly doesn't live here with you?" I asked Chava.

"Your mother says my Lilly would be an extra mouth for your grandfather to feed. Here, darling, your mother's word is law."

I could have taken this confession in stride, but it was Chava's utter candor that threw me off. I understood at once that it wasn't Grandpa's money that Chava was after, as my mother suggested. Nor was it a secure spot on Grandma Rose's carved mahogany bed. What Chava lusted after was territory for her Lilly.

At this time I was being groomed by my teacher, Miss Britton, for the coveted rapid Advance Class. If chosen, I would skip a grade. My parents were against my going into The Rapids, as they were known. Their expressed theory was that children should not be pushed to excel, but I knew that the true motive was a fear that my tantrums would grow worse. Although several physicians had assured my mother that I'd outgrow them, my mother was convinced that competition and pressure would only prolong my tantrums. Thus my parents adopted an attitude of benign neglect towards my scholarship.

How I envied the other students Miss Britton was grooming for The Rapids! How diligently their parents drilled them on their day's lessons! How vigorously they reviewed their homework assignments! Neatly crayoned construction paper covered their spotless tomes while my naked productions were smeared with careless ink blots.

That week, in honor of Brotherhood Week, Miss Britton had assigned each pupil to interview a relative on his or her country of origin. The assignment, which came close on the heels of the American victory in WWII, was eagerly anticipated by the class. The class prodigy, a girl of German ancestry, looked forward to a chance to bring her Bavarian family treasures. A polyglot bunch, the class provided a perfect ethnic mix for such a project. It was the most important week of the school year. Final decisions on The Rapids, it was rumored, would be made on the basis of the grades on the Brotherhood report.

I decided to avoid my parents entirely since they were next to useless when it came to help with school projects. That Saturday when we visited my Grandfather's house in Queens, I went straight to Grandpa at his rolltop desk on the sunporch and asked him where he was born. It seemed a reasonable way to begin.

"Who wants to know?" he answered in a gruff tone. Then he peered at me over his glasses, removed them, blew on each lens, removed his handkerchief from his pocket, cleaned each lens carefully and replaced the spectacles on his nose.

"It's for school," I replied.

"It's not anybody's business. Nobody should ask you that. Anyway, what's the use? It's all gone. Vanished."

"Please, Grandpa."

"Tell them you're as American as the next one," he said, and returned to making entries in his ledger book. I knew better than to press my grandfather when he was doing the books, so I decided to pose the question to my Uncle Phil, who knew everything about WWII, a true armchair general.

"Well, it's hard to say," replied my Uncle Phil in his lofty voice. "The territory changed hands so many times in history, darling, and each time its name changed, depending on who occupied it. It had one name when it was Poland and another when it was in Austro-Hungary. Then it was part of the Third Reich. Today I suppose it's the USSR."

I brooded over the answer. How could it vanish like smoke from a chimney or the stars at dawn? The labyrinth of modern European history set my head aching. There was only one place to turn to—Chava.

By suppertime my breath came only with difficulty and I began to feel anger clot my throat. My mother accused me of looking pale. Pallor was a sure sign that I was about to suffer one of my infamous tantrums. These were no ordinary tantrums; they seemed to arrive like demons, from nowhere. I tried everything to avoid a tantrum—holding my breath, banishing ugly thoughts, counting slowly from one to ten, to no avail. By bedtime I emitted an unrelenting barrage of howls and yelps. I refused to go to sleep before learning the exact name of Grandpa's birthplace. Otherwise The Rapids were closed to me forever. My mother refused to listen. My ears began to buzz. I turned red and threw myself onto the floor where I carried on by kicking and screaming.

My Uncle Phil lifted me up and carried me to bed. A thin trickle of pink snot ran from my nose into Chava's starched pillowcase. Shame fused to my mind like those forbidden colored sticks—ones from the penny candystore. I slept fitfully and woke from time to time to find the pillowcase damp from tears.

2

The following morning I crept down the stairs into Chava's kitchen where she was washing the pots and pans from the previous night's dinner in the double sink.

"Any better, darling?"

"Chava," I pleaded in a tiny voice, "I need to know the place where Grandpa was born." My voice must have signaled to her that it was a matter of life or death. I added that it was "for school", always an unassailable cause to Chava. I added that the report was due in just a few days and that my mother had refused to help.

She paused for a moment to consider and then a broad smile spread over her face. "Leave it to me," she said. "I'll find out." "But Grandpa said I'm an American."

She wrinkled up her nose and reassured me that she had her ways. Her eyes were as merry as little brown-and-mulberry wheels. Patting me tenderly, she gave me a sweet spoon to lick.

"Just one thing," she whispered to her co-conspirator. "Not a word to your mother. I don't want any more trouble from her." Solemnly, I promised Chava to keep our secret. All morning I kept glancing in her direction to see if our mission had succeeded. Just before our departure for The Bronx, she took me aside, her face flushed with excitement.

"I got the name," she whispered in my ear. Then she released the magical word.

Gradinga,

I made her say it again. She did. Then she shooed me away as my mother came into the room.

In the car on the way home, I kept saying the name to myself so I wouldn't forget it. It was an entirely agreeable sound, a word like Grandpa's hoarse accented Yiddish. It reminded me of barley or wheat waving in the wind, because it sounded like "grain." Or did it sound like "grading?" At any rate, I was delighted to be the proud possessor of a secret word. Despite the fact that it was coarse and rough to the tongue, I was certain that Miss Britton, with her fine intelligence, would find it quite suitable and could grasp at once the troubles I had endured in order to wrest it from my secretive family.

3

Brotherhood Day arrived. I rehearsed my precious word. The other children arrived armed with boxes of ornaments. Their schoolcases were crammed with boxes and bags. Out of these emerged dolls dresses in national costumes, trinkets, documents, books and all sorts of delicious baked goods. The voices of beautifully coached children delivering chronicles in loud confident voices chilled me with a foreboding sense of doom.. How could I ever hope to challenge the difficult Rapids with a spar as slender and ephemeral as a mere word—*Gradinga*. I slid down into my seat. The alphabetical roll call proceeded inexorably until my own name was called. Miss Britton looked down at me from beneath her gold-framed lenses. What had I to offer? I stared out of the window at the prisonlike courtyard and over the rooftops of the West Bronx. I knew at once that it was hopeless. Of what use was a single word that sounded like wind travelling through fields of barley or wheat? I looked up at her and meekly offered all I had. Then I watched in horror as an irritable Miss Britton scratched a "D" in the marking nook to commemorate my abysmal performance. After all, what was Gradinga when compared to yards of oratory, dioramas or costumed dolls?

At dismissal time I walked home alone, watching my righteous classmates in throngs of twos and threes discussing The Rapids. Even the familiar jingle of the Bungalow Bar man on his white truck failed to arouse any joy in me.

When my mother greeted me at the door, she had a worried expression on her face. I announced that I had no further plans to return to public school. In fact, I hated school, hated Miss Britton and the whole sixth grade, the whole world and everybody in it.

"What happened?" she asked.

It was too late for self-control. Rather than answer, she received a catastrophic noise like that of a dying beast. I told her nothing of my humiliations but instead began to look around the room for objects to hurl. For what seemed like hours, I stomped and screamed as if I suffered the tortures of the damned. Again she instructed me in various methods to ward off the tantrums. I ignored her foolish advice. Was the woman a total simpleton? Didn't she realize that these tantrums were beyond my control? Then she paced up and down in the hall and began to rave about the blood line, the genes, crazy Uncle Meyer, how I was a wild hyena, a *vilda chaya*, a child without a heart, a crazy lunatic. God would punish me. These predictions invariably prolonged the tantrums and made matters worse. Finally I lay down on the pillow and, after much fussing, allowed my mother to place a damp towel on my forehead. My nose bled all over the pillow, a sure sign that I was beginning to quiet down. That was the end of The Rapids for me.

That weekend when we visited my grandfather's house, Chava was eager to hear about my success at school with *Gradinga*. When I told her I had failed The Rapids for sure, she consoled me. "What's the rush anyway? Why do you need to skip a grade? You should enjoy your childhood. You have your whole life ahead of you."

"Doesn't your Lilly have to make reports at her school?" I asked.

Chava's face fell at the mention of Lilly. "I don't know, to tell you the truth. All I know is by her school they learn Yiddish and Hebrew."

"Lucky Lilly," I muttered.

"Why is she lucky?"

"She doesn't have to do reports for Brotherhood Week." I replied. Instinctively, I knew that trivia like baking and dressing dolls could not possibly occupy the mind of a Yiddish and Hebrew scholar like Lilly.

"She's not lucky," replied Chava, looking down at the apple strudel she was preparing.

"At least she doesn't have tantrums."

"You know, when I was a little girl, I was just like you. I had such a wild temper that my own mother said I was possessed of a dybbuk. What you call a devil. I was called a *vilda chaya,* just like you."

My eyes widened at the thought of a fellow sufferer. I thought I was the only unfortunate in the whole world to whom tantrums had been sent as a punishment. The confidential whisper in which Chava spoke immediately created a new bond between us. By then we had become companions in conspiracy.

"Listen to how I got cured. My mother brought me to this old Jewish woman who lived in a little hut in the middle of the forest. She told my mother it was only a little imp, not a big devil. Then she cured me by a secret charm to use against the Evil One. All you need is to do like me."

Chava demonstrated by inhaling several times until her cheeks puffed with air. They looked rounder than as if she had put a Spaldine in each one. Then she furiously worked saliva into her mouth. Slowly she let out the air and spat to the right (*Pfui!*) and to the left (*Pfui!*) and then in the middle (*Pfui!*) so hard I thought her teeth had been knocked out of her mouth.

"See?"

I nodded.

"Spit three times on the Evil One. Now you do it," she said. On subway platforms, signs prohibited spitting and warned miscreants of fines and arrests.

"Go ahead," said Chava. "Spit!" Finally I gathered enough saliva in my mouth to produce three weak, ladylike spits upon which Chava lavished extravagant praise. Now I was getting the hang of it.

"Are you sure this really works?" I asked.

"Of course I'm sure, It cured me, didn't it?"

"But here in New York?"

"Not by your mother's people. Not by the fancy-schmancey ladies on Mosholu Parkway with their noses stuck up in the air trying to act like Gentiles."

"Does it still work?"

"Even today on the Lower East Side old women practice the old charms and spells. Look at me and your Grandpa. Would we have met if not for the matchmaker?" Then she flushed and cast me a sideways smile.

Once again her eyes were those merry brown-and-mulberry wheels as they met my questioning ones. "It does no harm. If it helps, then it's good, no?"

4

It didn't take my mother long to notice my spitting habit. I was afraid of her hand coming down on me, but she didn't slap me. Instead she vowed to confront my mentor.

"Oh, that Chava! Teaching you those old *"bubbe meisehs."* Nothing but ignorant backward superstitions. I swear, I could kill her with my bare hands!"

I stared down at my laced brown oxfords. By implicating Chava I'd lost all honor. My mother further humiliated me by having a loud battle with Chava, after which I was forbidden to enter her kitchen. On those weekends in Queens when I peeked into her kitchen, Chava shooed me out with a dishtowel, saying she was already in enough hot water with my mother. It seemed I could do nothing right. Chava's remedies were old-country mumbo-jumbo to my mother and now I'd lost Chava's friendship.

On the last day of school I watched glumly as my classmates waved farewell, cheered on by their ambitious parents and marched off to the new junior high school after having skipped into The Rapids. Just as well! I was earning notoriety at school for being a troublemaker, which more than compensated for my slowness at my studies. My tantrums had been supplanted by a vengeful lust for mischief which I directed mainly at Miss Britton and other teachers. Not a day passed at school that I did not find some way to exact retribution and wreak revenge. I would make my parents rue the day that they had prevented me from skipping a grade.

5

On the hottest day of the summer, at the age of ninety-four, Great Aunt Bella passed away. Because of her charitable efforts in bringing refugees to America, her funeral was said to be a major occasion in the Jewish community. Fearful that I might misbehave at this solemn occasion, my mother capitulated and left me in Chava's care. Since Chava was only a relation by marriage, she was absolved of the necessity of attendance. Strict warnings from my mother were issued; I was not to get into mischief in her absence. As for Chava, my mother lifted her chin in an imperious gesture as she strode out the door in her black dress, hat and veil.

Once the door slammed, Chava uttered a sigh of relief. "Your mother doesn't like me, does she?" she said with a sneer.

"She says you're just telling me *bubbe meisehs.*"

"Maybe yes. Maybe no," said Chava enigmatically.

"What else can your magic charm do? Can it do anything else besides tantrums?"

Chava chuckled. "I wish it could, darling and so do others. Then they could have just spit Hitler into Hell."

A silence fell between us. Chava stopped her chopping and turned to me. Her voice was low and conspiratorial. "Tell me, I know your mother doesn't like me much, but doesn't she understand what happened to me and my Lilly by Hitler? Doesn't she know how I lost my whole family in Europe?"

I hunched my shoulders, unwilling to confess to Chava that my mother thought she was a *corva* or whore who was just after Grandpa's money. "She doesn't like to talk about Hitler," I said.

"Doesn't she talk about the extermination of the Jews? About the ovens? The death camps?" Her eyes pierced mine.

"She doesn't like when I ask too many questions."

"About the Jews? You never heard about the crematoria? Where they gassed millions of Jews?" Her tone of voice was incredulous. When she saw my innocent face, she threw up her hands and began to implore the ceiling in Yiddish. What kind of a woman would refuse to tell a Jewish child what had happened to other Jews in Europe? What my parents had tried to spare, Chava felt was essential knowledge for a Jewish child. The Holocaust, which had been a fuzzy shadow, now began to assume a definite outline as Chava launched into a description in her broken English of Hitler's war against the Jews.

For the first time I heard of boxcars, showers, gas, ovens, ashes, gold fillings from teeth and other atrocities. In my mother's version, we had only reached the point at which Hitler was sending Jews off to work in labor camps. Now as Chava spoke, I began to understand the fate of those nameless relations on the other side, the ones Great Aunt Bella had tried to save. When Chava finished, I began to put together missing pieces in the jig-saw puzzle that was the well-kept secret of the Holocaust. I had always suspected that there was more to it than our schoolteachers taught us and more than my mother wanted me to know. Now I began to comprehend my grandfather's refusal to unearth the past. Miss Britton's Brotherhood Day. My uncle's lofty explanations. My mother's silences. My father's collaboration. The vanished town of Gradinga. The borders that shifted and the town that changed names.

"All the Jews?" I asked.

"Yes, my dear, Even schoolgirls like you, babies even. And only because they were Jews. This is something every American child should learn."

All of my mother's evasions began to appear as interconnected parts in some great conspiracy to spare me the truth and to keep me ignorant of the full extent of the terror Hitler had unleashed against the Jews. As Chava lit the old-fashioned stove and slid in the navy enamel roasting pan, I inhaled a whiff of kitchen gas and began to flail my arm about.

"*Gas! Gas!*" I cried, holding my nose.

Just at that moment I heard the front door open and a herd of black-clad relatives entered the parlor, followed by my parents. They found me on the floor in the throes of a tantrum. My mother lifter her black veil and peered into my eyes. Then she turned to Chava "What have you been doing?"

"I told you no good could come of leaving those two together." She told my father. Then she turned back to me and began to try to coax the tantrums away by having me count to ten. I then began to suspect my mother of cataloguing under "*bubbe meiseh*" not just Hitler's extermination of the Jews, but other truths as well. What other hideous secrets did her untrustworthy smile conceal? As for my father, what sins did his silence cover?"

"What has Chava been telling you?" demanded my mother as she stood over my prostrate form. I could barely distinguish her words, which sounded as if she were shouting to me through a thick concrete tunnel, her voice at once muffled yet amplified.

"I told her about Hitler's extermination of the Jews. It's time she found out. She's a Jewish child."

"My Hannah doesn't need a history lesson from a greenhorn," said my mother angrily.

"You can't keep it from her forever", interjected a relative.

"I can tell her myself," replied my mother with an imperious lift of her chin. "My poor mother Rose, she should rest in peace, died upstairs in the bedroom coughing her guts out so that this refugee could give orders in her house? Not over my dead body!" My mother's tirade caused a pall of silence to fall over the room.

Pretending to swoon, I tossed my body from side to side. I rummaged through my mind for a way to prolong the attention. It occurred to me that I was play-acting, that I was really lying under the ground, like the Jewish children in Europe and I could really stop kicking and flailing if I wanted. For a second I commanded myself, "Stop!" And I stopped. The sheer joy of knowing that I had the power to command my body filled me with a new courage. From my place on the floor, the room whirled around like a pinwheel in front of my eyes. The white of the stove blended with the floral pattern on Grandam Rose's dishes and the chocolate misery of Chava's eyes matched the dark hem of my mother's mourning dress.

Finally I opened one to find Chava kneeling above. She coaxed me to rise. I sat up and watched her. She puffed up her mouth so that it looked as large as the Hindenburg and motioned me to do the same. Mesmerized by her facial gestured, I worked my tongue around my mouth until I was able to coax up some spittle in the far recesses of my mouth. As she pretended to produce the forbidden formula, I followed. To the left (a weak *pfu*!) and to the right (a weak *pfui*!) then to the center. A stream of yellow snot augmented the spit that flew from my lips to the floor.

6

My sudden recovery was like a badge of honor for Chava. All night she kept cutting me slices of her strudel, for I was now her vindication and proof of her special powers in the house.

Shortly after I was cured of my tantrums, a metal folding cot appeared in the corner of the large kitchen. When I asked, my mother replied that this cot was for Chava's girl, Lilly, who was moving from Rivington Street to Grandpa's house to help her mother with the housework. One Sunday in early September, Lilly arrived, looking like a proper lady with her Shirley Temple curls and dimples. I don't know why, but in the weeks that followed, my tantrums died out and ceased to be a subject for either mystery or reproach. The pitifully thin mattress of the cot was full of lumps but Lilly didn't seem to notice. Within weeks of her arrival, Lilly covered the wall above her bed with pictures of movie stars neatly scissored from screen magazines. Grandpa didn't seem to notice. Even my mother's mouth clamped shut.

That year, at Succoth, rain hung in the air like a promise. It thundered at night but Chava whistled merrily to herself in the kitchen, for she had gained her territory at last.

SPARING THE CHILDREN
Barbara Unger

We dug in the park
for buried treasure,
secret caches left by pirate bands,
unearthed shards of bottles,
flints, pennies,
the deposits
of our history.

But the Holocaust was a well-kept secret
on the broad boulevards of The Bronx.

Our parents edited war news
so it wouldn't disturb our dreams
of perfect report cards
or cast a rancid smell
over our home life, hanging
like a damp overcoat
in the hall closet.

We swallowed war communiqués
with Hershey bars and egg creams,
Watched Hitler move like a jerky puppet
across the Movietone screen.

Our fathers tamed the death camps
with tales of factories and schools
where children wearing sewn-on stars
learned by German rules.

Our mother snipped along the ribs
of the truth, with room to let out
in a year or so, since children grow.

They pinned our hems, stitched in gussets,
scissored out box cars, gas chambers,
the ovens of Auschwitz...

until at last they could censor the facts
no more and we learned to dig up these crimes
and hold the horror in our hands.

Figure 1.4   Leah Korica   "Our Bones Don't Belong to Us"

TWIN
Hannah Stein

> "... *we still love life...we still hope, hope about everything*"
> Anne Frank

How could you have died: I
would have sensed it.
Without having seen you
I know you are the one
who suffered, who was made to touch
the dead. Your mouth was filled
with stones. It was you who tore
giving birth, I who only knew
something was tearing. We have caught
the same fevers at the same
moment: we wait to become real
to one another.

They would have taken me as I sat
on a stone bench in a desolate yard
or walked quickly with a younger
brother through byways, hurrying
to a neighbor's root cellar
or upstairs annex. You and I were ten
the year they crossed the border.
I've seen the story in glossy black and white:
old women at the ice cart buying fish
wrapped in a tattered paper. Once
while delivering bread for grandmother

you heard a piano. You stayed
beneath the rich man's windows,
made yourself late to dinner:
faces around the big table
joyous, though rumors
sizzled like meat beneath their songs.

At the same moment that I
sat at my school desk, you were grasped
by the collar. Flung to earth, a soldier
in a greatcoat. Bruises
on your thighs. While I repeated

"je suis, tu es." I am. You were.
In the schoolyard
I cried: the boy who hated me
spat in my face, cursed
my mothers and fathers
In that instant you

could have been taken out of time.
Or not: you might have fought.
Or escaped during the thirty days.
Changed sides, married one of them.
Maybe you always wear long sleeves
to hide a number. I think

you keep moving as I do,
throw the shuttle of your eyes
back and forth over faces, certain
that someday you will look
and recognize yourself. At night
or in a pondering of light.
When jagged parts seal over. When
it becomes hard to keep the beat.
By now we've traveled far, rag after rag
thrown down with toothbrushes,
with shoes and tins of shoe polish
still there, in mythic quantities. Small
heroic objects. And when I see them
when I see the pictures
from the camps

I don't marvel that I live, but ask
which one is me?

SILENT NIGHT
Joan Lipkin

I have this melancholy that kicks in like the flu around Christmas and lingers the year 'round. It's when I watch everybody around me behaving like a Hallmark card and I'm nowhere near the frame. I know in my heart that not everybody's that happy. Maybe the guy in the Santa Claus hat hits his wife. Or the kids in their matching red flocked ice skating outfits go home to an empty house. But it looks like everyone is celebrating a Kodak moment. Everyone else but me.

So you might say that I was doomed before I even met Jim. Tall. Blonde. Irish Catholic. And Male. Everything that I'm not. Besides, the boys where I was from had names like Sam. Ira. Howard. How could I go out with them? They had names like my father. They were my father.

It was the fall of my senior year, in between borrowing the car and choosing a direction for my own life. My father was so pleased that I had been selected to speak at graduation. At dinner, he used to sit at the head of our heavy oak table, looking drained and angry, daring us to rouse him from his exhaustion with our brilliance.

"What did the President know and when did he know it? Quick.. Quick..

Like knowing the day's events would erase the tattoo on my second cousin's forearm.

The memory of the Holocaust hung heavy as furniture wax in our house. Maybe it was about leaving home, but that summer the night-mares came back as I imagined they were coming for me. After all, didn't I look just like my Grandma Hannah, everybody said.

My father's answer was for us to be smarter. Quicker. More verbal. "I expect my children to be exceptional," he said.

But I didn't want to be exceptional. I wanted to eat Chef Boy-R-Dee from cans instead of my mother's carefully planned meals. To call my father Pops like they did on the Patty Duke Show and loll about on the floor like a dumb teenager. To disappear into a crowd of average.

What if I said the wrong thing, I asked him silently, wrapping my hair tightly in orange juice cans to look like the girls who lived safely within the pages of Seventeen Magazine. What then ?

With Jim, I began to plan my escape. Maybe I could have a life different from the one I had been handed. Hey, this is America. Isn't that why my mother braved the long boat ride from Poland? So there could be a choice?

The day of the Christmas party, I lied to my mother and said we were going to a concert.

"But it's the first night of Hanukkah" she protested, trying not to look hurt.

"Look, we've had these tickets for weeks," I said. "And it's not like we don't have all those other nights."

She let it drop, and turned her attention to polishing the already gleaming menorah. We were careful around each other for the rest of the day, neither one sure what the etiquette of betrayal and rejection should look like.

As I walked into the party, the wreath on the door seemed to wink at me. Maybe I could pull this thing off. Always a good student, I had studied well, trading my usual tie-dyed tee shirt and jeans for a navy blue calf length dress. From a distance, it would be hard to pick me out in a lineup.

Jim smiled and handed me a glass of eggnog. My eyes buzzed. "You don't think I can get through this family scene without a little help," he said, gesturing at a sea of similar faces.

I thought of my younger sister curled up in front of the television doing her algebra homework and my father who was probably squinting over the financial page and figuring out how to pay for three unexpected sets of braces.

"Merry Christmas," someone said. "Merry Christmas," I said back, tasting the words that I had heard so often but had never said. Someone else called me Kathleen. Jim's previous girlfriend.

"She doesn't look anything like Kathleen," he snapped.
"What does Kathleen look like?" I asked.
"Oh, you know…different."

Questions always made me thirsty. So did the nut studded cheeseball. I thought he said there would be dinner.

Someone—I think it was Jim's cousin Betsy—asks how long I have known him. Someone—I think it was Jim's brother Hank—asks where I go to school. Someone—I'm sure it was his mother—asks where my family lives.

"Hey," Jim said, coming to my rescue. "What's with the third degree?"

"It's okay," I said, teetering in my new high heels as I backed up into the tree. The hot ring of lights felt like barbed wire. "They don't know me."

Then the singing began and they turned toward each other. I checked my hair in the mirror over the highboy in the front hallway. It was starting to frizz.

> Silent Night
> Holy night
> All is calm
> All is bright

Jim squeezed my hand the way he had squeezed my breast three hours earlier in the front seat of his sky blue Ford Pinto.

"Did I forget to tell you? Everybody gets to solo," he whispered in my ear. "It's kind of corny, I know, but my Dad likes to show off. You don't mind do you?"

> Round yon virgin
> Mother and child
> Holy infant so tender and mild

Mind? I had waited my whole life to sing this song. I gazed into the large crackling fire and tried not to think of my family gathered around their tiny flame.

> Sleep in heavenly peace
> Sleep in heavenly peace

Surely I know the words. They had been piped into every elevator and shopping mall and radio station since I could remember. My mother had even taken us for a holiday breakfast downtown at Saks one time until she realized it meant pancakes and sausages and sitting on Santa's lap. My beautiful, curly haired mother who was home right now, watching Walter Cronkite on the nightly news while she made a holiday dinner that I wouldn't be there to eat.

> Silent night
> Holy night
> Shepherd's quake
> at the sight

I leaned in towards the singing blonde circle, where everything seemed easy and casual because they took for granted their right to be there. And as the solo shifted from Jim's sister Mary to his brother Hank, I wondered, were these the secret passwords?

> Glory streams from heaven above
> Heavenly hosts sing alleluia!

But as I began to sing, my tongue suddenly felt thick as pickled herring, my eyes filled with salt. "Go for it, babe," Jim whispered. "Then we can get out of here and have some, you know, real fun."

> Christ our savior is born
> Christ our savior is born.

As everyone smiled expectantly at me, I sat in horror at the eternal silence a few seconds can hold. Then, slowly, from somewhere came a voice that sounded like my own.

> *Bo-ruh a-toh a-do-nay*
> *e-lo-hey-nu me-leh ho-olom*
> *a-sher ki-d'sho-nu b'mits-vo-tov*

As I sang, first softly, then louder, my hands flew out of my lap, like birds released from their cage. I watched them, as I had watched myself enter the room in my new blue dress. No, this was not Kathleen. It was my mother. My grandmother. My Aunt Sadie who was married to a pattern cutter on the lower east side of New York.

> *V'tsi-vo-nu*
> *l'had-leek neyr*
> *shel Hanukkah.*

I dropped my punch glass. The crystal cup that had been in this country longer than my family.

"It's alright, dear," Jim's mother said, dabbing at the pale spreading stain. "These things happen." Jim's brother Hank snickered. Jim stood looking puzzled, as he rubbed one foot against the other.

"No, it's not," I said. "I'm sorry. And I want to go home." And as I mouthed the words of that ancient prayer, I knew I was home.

II.

Through the Eyes of a Child

from THE HIDDEN CHILD

Susan Terris

One time, when meat was scarce,
those who concealed us
rode their bicycles past Sunday soccer
to dig up tulip bulbs.
We roasted them, peeled the brown,
and ate them. As I chewed,
I thought *tulip, tulip* and tried to let
the flower I could not see
bloom inside.

THE SEASONS OF THE SWASTIKA
Henny Wenkart

the first swastika season
I was four
little biplanes flew over vienna
and from them
colored little paper swastikas
fluttered down like petals in the blossom season.

I stuffed my pockets full of blue, pink, orange thin-angled petals,
tried to stuff the glorious carpet of paper petals
from the sidewalk all into my pockets.
That was a sin, I could see that as soon as I got them home.
Mitzi laughed, but her laugh was wrong,
and mommy shook me! Screamed at Mitzi!
Picked me up and shook me!

The second time those petals came
I never touched one.
I was ten years old
And I never touched them.

The first swastika season
daddy held a lawyer's pass to the inner city
we could make our Sunday outing to the palace garden
daddy had a pass

young soldiers in pairs let us through
to this pass only the palace itself was off limits.
Still, I tantrummed for my climbing ledge along the palace wall
and serenely, his hair shining, his smile
shining,
daddy approached the sergeant: "do you
have a little child? What can I do?
She always climbs there…

the first swastika season I won.

The second time they bloomed
Blood red and black
Down the buildings,
On people's arms,
High on the church steeples against the sky.
I never touched them.

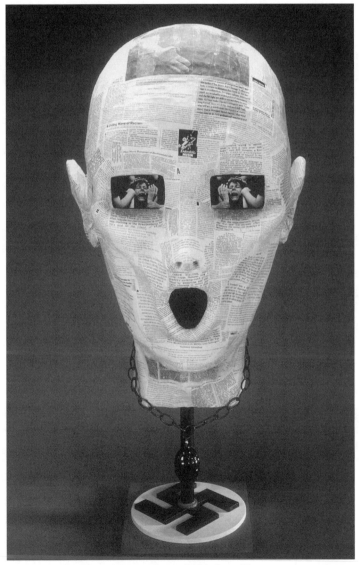

Figure 2.1   Harold Lewis   "Skinhead"

BECOMING A JEW
Myra Sklarew

When I was born
they called me a Jew.
I hurried to put on
the shoes
of a Jew. I hurried
to put on the hat
of a Jew. But still
I wasn't a Jew.
In the mirror I tried
to read the difference
between us. But my red
hair, my pale skin
refused to explain it.
They asked if I
believed in their God.
I put a star
on a chain at my neck
but like the dress
of my sister
it did not fit.
They gave my sister
a cloth badge
and she sewed it on
with perfect stitches,
with fine black thread.
They took my sister
away to the center
of our city and left
her there without food
or water. For seven days.
We did not see
my sister again.
The young boys began
sailing their bodies
through the glass
windows like kites.

My father's tears
on the stone step.
My father's name.

Figure 2.2   Lisa Kokin   "Unearthing" (detail)

Figure 2.3   Lisa Kokin   "Unearthing"

THE HIDDEN CHILD
Susan Terris

I was good. We were all good
Dutch children—those of us
who survived.

Before the Nazis, *Moeder* brandished
other threats—potatoes that would grow
behind unwashed ears, rats
that might nest in unkempt hair.
Then jackboots on cobblestone began
to punctuate days and nights.
In our attic room, no soccer balls
or bicycles, no tulips: and sometimes
we ate dog meat to survive.

My daughter asks about the taste.
I say I don't remember.
She probes what I mean by good:
How good is good, she wonders,
keen to quantify. Imagining me
studious, parsing out days
for later profit, she cannot fathom
the card games, flatness, waste.
She says I'm hooded, use
time as a weapon. It is. It was . . .

One time, when meat was scarce,
those who concealed us
rode their bicycles past Sunday soccer
to dig up tulip bulbs.
We roasted them, peeled the brown,
and ate them. As I chewed,
I thought *tulip, tulip* and tried to let
the flower I could not see
bloom inside.

Last year when the hidden ones met,
I did not go. I told my daughter
I was out of time.

Figure 2.4   Rosa Naparstek   "If Love Had Wings" (detail)

Figure 2.5 Chandra Garsson "Persephone"

April 1943: BORSZCZOW
Myra Sklarew

Only you little collarbutton dared
to sing in death's courtyard: *the Jews know*
nothing yet they walk
in the marketplace at noon they are hauled
to the graveyard they kneel down say
goodbye to the whiteness of light the dead
no longer care what they wear the others
carelessly wearing their clothes Spinka little collar
button when I lie down on the earth
is it you I hear still singing
to that scattered remnant or were you buried
alive in their courtyard for loving them

MURRAY'S STORY
Gary Pacernick

When I was a boy on the train
To Auschwitz, it took twelve days.
There was nothing to eat.
After a while you don't feel hungry
But the thirst is terrible.
Then someone found a tin can.
We cut a hole in it, took a piece
Of string and tied it through
That hole. We dangled the can out
Of the train until we brought back
Some snow. Then we licked drops
Of moisture from that icy snow.
I was just a small boy on this cattle car,
But when I think back to it
I get thirsty; my lips and mouth
Feel parched. Sometimes when snow is
On the ground, I pick up a handful
And put it to my lips as I did on that train
To Auschwitz when I was so thirsty
I felt that I was going to die.

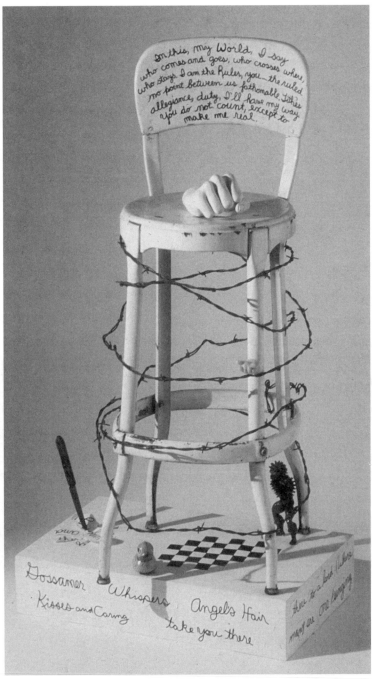

Figure 2.6   Rosa Naparstek   "The Order of Things"

Figure 2.7　Barbara Milman　"Auschwitz #6"

THE YOUNGEST KNOWN
HOLOCAUST SURVIVOR
Charles Fishman

for Dani and Haya

At 3, she was caged above the ovens
a twin with her twin sister: small wooden cage
no windows   Only Mengele held the key
and opened that darkness to the flames
What he needed was their bones and their pain
whiter than the first flare of light after blindness
Who could she cling to but her sister
who shuddered and gulped death in the darkness
who stuttered her name which was *Sora*
so that to soothe herself *Sora* she could only
stammer back? And when she died
in her own arms Mengele broke her fingers
What can survive this death which comes
pouring out of her even now? Only the twin
of her anger   the twin of her sorrow.

MOTHER HUNGER
Chana Bloch

1

Every knothole was a branch once.

The way her face dissolved
that time she went away: *I have to go, I have to*
his swollen *no, mama!* his wet
hands pulling
at her woolen skirt. He had to

stand there
stand there forever with the hired auntie and watch
as car after car of the long train
turned into steam.
Don't cry. You're a big boy now.

And then she was
back again, white-faced
mother of sorrows. A shriek at the window,
a worry on the shelf like a Meissen vase
a child mustn't break.

2

How the heat scatters her. A sudden whip
of wind. Here and there a bristly growth,
narrow leaves flinching.

They live in one close room,
a nest of flaking
newspapers. To have come
to this. Ten steps from bed
to dresser. Another five
to the door. And the child
clouding and polishing his face
in the family spoons.

Figure 2.8 Denise Satter   "Madonna and Child"

Her child, after all. *You are my*
Everything, she whispers,
and he nods.
Then that thirst rises in her—
                              She buries
her mouth in his cheek, his neck.

In the green bowl: heaped oranges,
the casual abundance of that other life.

3

Terrible always to be teetering
on stilts, those small wooden platforms
six inches off the ground.
He won't ever walk gracefully
though he is learning not to fall.

The applause that comes like a full stop
at the end of a sentence
is reward, or almost.
Still, he has to beg for it.

He wants to go down to the pond
after school like the others
and fish for tadpoles.
He'll take them home in a biscuit tin
with moss and water, a few twigs
to keep them company—
                              But there is papa
waving his arms again, shouting:
You must not worry mama.
And there is mama.

To live in their gaze
is to live in a house of glass.
Wherever he looks out
a severe love presses at the pane
looking in.

4

The child a palimpsest of his parents'
losses, each one slapped over
the last—wet paint of
swastikas on the windows
of that two-hundred-year-old house
and the money the maid stole
to help them get out and mama's
But if we get caught?—
red *J* of the passports, stamped
in the sweat of their hands.

Then that land of promises where the heat
flays the houses
where grass burns to khaki dust in the sun
where papa pedals uphill and
falls off the bike
dead at ten in the morning
just because it's over doesn't mean
it stops happening
and mama's still a little Ida in pigtails
crying in the corner.

He raises a puzzled face for her
pitying kiss. She's waiting for him.
It's her grief that flashes across
his old night sky. His hands shake
as hers did the year she died, he can't
hold a glass or write
his name on the line. Her terror
grips him. He turns
the soiled pages of his book
with her clumsy wet thumb.

THE REFUGEE CHILD MEETS HER FATHER EUGENE AT WAR'S END
Liliane Richman

Teacher's talking with a stranger
in the courtyard
while we count our sticks
three green ones minus
two red equal . . .

then she returns calling my name.
Lydia come meet your father
The world tumbles inside my head
I twist the bottom of my dress

I already got a father
he rides his bicycle to work
wears a beret
his face glows in the sun
unlike this pale man
who takes my hand
squeezes tight
He walks so fast

And at home they say
Look what your daddy brought
all this candy for you
Then I clap my hands,
though all of this is hearsay
I remember nothing about separations

One day I leave the red and white countryhouse
for the city and grow to love the stranger
and his sickly wife my birth mother
just returned from the concentration camp

Then we live in a cramped apartment
there are also brothers.
all of us strangers
rescued from fires.

MEMORANDUM, 1945
A FAMILY REUNITED
Liliane Richman

How handsome my father
Gypsy king,
coal eyes unsmiling
How beautiful my mother
seagreen in her pupils
her demi-ingenue smile
a five pointed boutonniere
resting on her chest
above the just recovered girl child
serious and starched all in white
puzzled by the photographer
who tells these family members
made strangers by the unreason of the world
to watch the little bird

Figure 2.9   Chandra Garsson   "Maya II"

DREAMS OF A NUNNERY
Odette Meyers

In this passage from Doors to Madame Marie, *Odette, 12, confronts her parents whose shattered Jewish world she had re-entered two years earlier from her wartime immersion in deeply Catholic rural life. Like other Jewish children in post-war Paris, constantly reminded of how lucky she was since she hadn't died in camp, she was urged to "get back to normal." But what did "normal" mean if you had just turned five when the war started, seven when you were suddenly torn from your family to live with strangers as a secret Jew and an open Catholic, almost ten when you were just as suddenly thrown back into a broken Jewish world to be both a tormented and proud Jew and a secretly devoted Catholic? Unable to reconcile her two identities, the girl longs for the serene, simple, dependable routine of a nunnery. It seems infinitely easier to follow vows and rules and say set prayers than to try to understand what had happened to her family, her people, how the Holocaust had turned them into ashes, then stories, photos, ghosts...*

I had to get back to Paris. I did so smuggling presents from my host family. André had given me one of his tiny bottles of holy water from Lourdes and his parents had bought me a wooden rosary. Back home, I hid the gifts under my pillow and otherwise quickly resumed my former life. Secretly, though, I recited the rosary when no one was home, sometimes took the subway to faraway neighborhoods where no one knew me so I could however briefly and gingerly enter a church, and at all times I dreamed of my future in the convent. Whenever I received a letter from André's uncle, I read it several times to make sure I didn't miss a single instruction. To my disappointment, each letter still advised patience: plans had to be made carefully so nothing would go wrong. Aside from patience, prayers and good deeds were highly recommended to help advance the cause. And in my prayers, I should not forget to pray for the souls of my parents, those non-believers who as such played in the hands of Satan.

I hid the letters under my pillow, with the bottle of holy water and the wooden rosary.

One early week-day evening, much to my surprise, both my parents came home. I wondered what the occasion was. "We want to talk to you," my mother said sternly, setting up three chairs in the dining-area. Two of them were side-by-side and the third at a polite distance across from them. My father had gone into the bedroom and as he came back, I could see him slip something into his pants pocket. He sat down on one of the two chairs, the one closer to the table with my mother next to him closer to the kitchen, and motioned to me to sit down on the third chair. Formalities between us in our own home? It did not bode well! I sat silently, waiting anxiously for the next move from my parents.

As usual my mother was the one to break the silence. She was furious. "How can you? After all we did for you! For this we got through the war?" I didn't understand. She made herself clearer though she nearly choked on the words: "How can you? How can you have a correspondence with that priest? He says we're under the spell of Satan! How can you go along with such slander? About your own mother, your own father? How can you? How?"

If she had thrown a bucket of ice water at my face, it would have had the same affect: I would have awakened with a start and stuttered with sudden realizations: she had discovered my "Catholic" hiding, she was reading my letters, I had no privacy, why did she pick on that one phrase about Satan, why didn't she see how important it was for me to become a nun? Why?

My father then took my rosary out of his pocket, held it up contemptuously and asked me if I realized the true symbolism of that object. I was going to answer but he told me to be quiet, he was doing the talking. And he did, going into an elaborate analysis of how the Catholic church's treatment of Jews had led to vicious anti-Semitism which led to genocide at Auschwitz and elsewhere. And how could I, a Jewish daughter, so betray my own people? How could I? Everyone had put themselves out to save me, and here I did survive and I even had both my parents alive. They were working hard for me . . .

I wanted to try to defend myself, to explain how orderly and peaceful life would be in a nunnery, how it wouldn't cost them anything, how I would never be a burden to them, how I would pray for them and for every single Jew, dead or alive. But I was too slow. My parents were taking turns speaking angrily, accusingly at me, ending up with questions of me but not waiting for an answer. Their duo performance picked up speed; they interrupted each other; they spoke faster, louder. I turned my head to one then the other. I was getting dizzy. They were going too fast. I was rapidly falling behind in my understanding till finally I lost it . . . Their words had a sound to them but it was as if I had become deaf to what was inside, or behind, or around those words. I just turned my head to one parent then to the other and again as if I were shaking my head no, no, no.

When the meaning of the words no longer reached me, I turned and turned to the source of the major sound, looking at the face that went with it, first one then the other. And I was increasingly overcome with immense affection for those familiar faces, those proud, passionate Jewish faces of my mother, my father, both so dear to me! It was so wonderful to sit across from them, to have them together, like this, all to myself! It was even better than the occasional meal eaten together: here we were not distracted by food. There wasn't even a table between us. Just empty space. Formal space. Oh but it hurt, that space between us! I wished their chairs would slide forward of their own volition so my parents could be within touching distance. They were still making a lot of gestures but as time went on, they spoke more softly. Maybe it was fatigue, or maybe they had said everything they wanted to say - very quickly at first then slower, as one eats too fast when one is too hungry. As they softened, so did my love for them, my mother, my father. I could cover them with a feather quilt of love. At the same time, my longing for their love grew more urgent: I wished they would get up, right then, each in turn, breach that formal space between us to stand by my chair, then bend down and kiss me on both cheeks with an endearing word in between. I couldn't bear that space between us . . .

Something very strange has just happened: there is a silence. Why? Where am I? What am supposed to be doing? I must have stared at my parents in bewilderment because my mother was asking me very kindly: "Do you understand now?" I said yes because her voice was so kind though I wasn't sure what I was supposed to understand: I had missed so much of the explanation.

My father then asked me if I would answer any more letters from the Grangier family and I could see him hold his breath with solemn anxiety. I said no because I didn't want him to be anxious.

By then the space between us was no longer so forbidding. Soon, I had one of those brief moments of absolute happiness that taste of eternal bliss: I was with both my mother and my father; I had their complete attention. They must have forgiven me all my transgressions. They were desperate for me not to leave them for the nunnery but to stay with them. My little family!

Again, my father was dangling my rosary. Now I stared at it as at an enemy. I was furious with myself. I had let it happen: I was taken in. I had lost my bearing. I had betrayed my secular upbringing. Worst of all, I had almost let them take me away from my parents, hide me into a convent without their knowledge! What would they have done when they would have noticed my absence? I hadn't thought of it before. Surely they would have called the police. Surely they would have been hysterical with grief and they would have cried: "For that we survived the war?" Didn't the priest think of all this? What kind of religion did he represent?

Separating children from their parents! He was evil. I was seized by a hard hatred of that priest - Satan in disguise. Nobody, not that man, not anyone, ever will separate me from my mother, my father. No one.

My father got up, still holding my rosary. "All right," he said, "that's settled," and he motioned for me to follow him. I did just that. He led me to the tiny toilet-room, opened the door, gave me the rosary and ordered me to throw it in the toilet. I did. Then I pulled the cord to flush it down.

FOR THE JEWISH BABY IN THE WARSAW GHETTO
Leatrice Lifshitz

You were in the wrong place
at the wrong time.

A bed. A room. A house.
What was that for a Jewish baby?

A name. A hand. A smile . . .

Even less.

A mother. A father.
A kiss. A cry. A howl.

A God

Yes, even less . . .

You should have been born to a mountain
grown sturdy in a cave

or possibly a tunnel
with a light at the end of it

slept soundly on stone

playing with whatever ripples
you could find

slipping into morning
as if it were

a bridge

a basket . . .

Figure 2.10   Chaim Goldberg   "Star of David"

Yes, we remember where
it once was

a basket and a baby

floating at the right place
at the right time . . .

Figure 3.1   Harley Gaber   "Die Plage"

III.

Survival

THE SURVIVORS ARE DYING
Charles Fishman

What is a fire without a witness?
Mountains sleep in anonymous
beauty, the earth vegetates—luxuriant
coma!—and death tracks its millions.

They are dying, those who lived
when snow was thirst embodied
and dry crust was a feast of lights
and murder was the blessing
that ushered in the meal.

What is the smell of death
without the gift of witnesses
without the histories written
in their blood?

Figure 3.2   Deborah Trilling   "They Say I Have Her Bones"

THE WIDOW AND DAUGHTER
Irena Klepfisz

"The widow Rose and small daughter Irena survived and now reside
in New York." Translated from the Yiddish in *Doyres Bundistn* (Generations of Bundists).

The widow
a shadow of the wife Rose
       (he was over six feet
       and called her *Mala*,
       little one)
at one time expected
to live
       not survive.

In those days
she was romantic
       (they met one winter
       when he chased
       and overtook her on a ski slope.)
She read many novels,
knew all the love songs
       (one in particular
       was her favorite—
       ja nie jestem winna,
       it's not my fault)
knew the first part
of *Pan Tadeusz* by heart,
helped her husband
with his work
       (he was an engineer
       and she drew circles for him
       with a protractor)
and never believed
that he might die
       (he was a champion jumper
       and discus thrower)
but would be young always

in their apartment in Warsaw
      (it was sometimes called
      she told me proudly
      the little Paris of Eastern Europe)
where she would receive her sisters,
nieces, nephews (one of the twins died)
and dreamed into a mist even grandchildren
of unborn sons and daughters
and looked forward to intellectual discussions
about the progress of the workers' movement,
the latest romance in a novel or the family.

Instead she survived
motherhood
      (she was in labor for three days,
      and then he said: something has to be done)
the Aryan side
      (she became a maid
      and was polishing silver for *them*
      while the ghetto burned)
widowhood
      (as a child I asked
      if she cried a lot
      when they told her
      and she said
      yes)
and finally New York
      (she became a dressmaker
      and did alterations)
with the little daughter
product of three days of labor
a moving monument
whose melted existence
formed an eternal flame
(at memorial meetings
she lit candles
for all the children
who had perished).

These two:
widow and half-orphan
survived and now resided
in a three-room apartment
with an ivy-covered fire escape
which at night
clutched like a skeleton
at the child's bedroom wall.

To this apartment
which chained them
welded them
in a fatal embrace
the missing one
returned at night.

The missing one
was surely
the most
        important
link.

He held out on the fire escape
refusing to give up
his strategic position.
He was there
on the wall
with his whole family
staring out of the picture,
on the piano
staring out of the picture,
in the living room
(vying with her mother for attention)
staring out of the picture,
till the apartment
seemed to burst with his eyes
which penetrated every corner
seizing every movement of their mouths
and made them conscious

that he understood
every word they spoke.

And when the two crowded
into the kitchen at night
he would press himself between them
pushing, thrusting, forcing them to remember,
even though he made his decision,
had chosen his own way
rather than listening to the pleas of her silence
  (she once said: I never complained about his activities
  and Michal said he was glad I was not like other wives
  who wanted to draw their husbands back into safety)
he would press himself between them—
hero and betrayer
legend and deserter—
so when they sat down to eat
they could taste his ashes.

NATURAL HISTORY
Roald Hoffmann

In Block 18 is the professor from Amsterdam
traded his shirt for a stub of a pencil
and school notebook, ruled in sections

for beating, by implement—rifle butt, hose
or hand; transgressions of the Hippocratic Oath;
making people watch death, by kind of death;

making people steal. Not to remember, he said,
but to learn, the way in 1652 Menasseh
ben Israel listed demons—possessors, imps,

snatchers of purses and cats, poltergeists,
dybbuks, child killers—evil put in order,
like Brazilian vipers, inventoried, soon

understood. Before they took him to the KB
he paid Jean two crusts to guard the book. Who
sold it, page by page, for rolling cigarettes.

SOUP
Enid Dame

for Josh Waletszsky

1.
I am making chicken soup in the Vilna Ghetto.
You think it's easy? First
you've got to sneak in the chickens
feather by feather   bone by bone   and then the vegetables
root by root   leaf by leaf   next, the salt
past the Jewish police at the gate, and the Lithuanians,
the Nazis over their shoulders. You've got to be careful.
I keep the soup pot alive in the Vilna Ghetto
while all around buildings simmer
with meetings: young people, Zionists, leftists, rightists,
Communists, Bundists. My brother
tells me I'm on the wrong track.

He is sneaking guns into the Vilna Ghetto
part by part   scrap by scrap   and then the explosives.
This isn't easy, he says, but it's necessary.
Think of the working class, think of the revolution.
Think of the heroes at Warsaw, think of the pits at Ponar.
All we need here is a little solidarity.
All we need now is one good uprising.

2.
She is sneaking Jews out of the Vilna Ghetto
into the forest   man by man   woman by woman
(there are no children left, no Jewish children).
The leader, a Jew with a Russian name, "Yurgis,"
doesn't like it at all.
But what can he do?
She is a hero, I guess. Here she is on TV,
on the documentary my daughter watches.

Me, I was somewhere nearby. I was making soup in the forest
for the Partisans, the peasants, the Jews, the Russians.
(I left my brother, he left me, back in the ghetto.)
Here, we trapped some rabbits, dug up a few wild scallions.
Yadwiga found us some mushrooms.
(They looked poisonous, but tasted like pine trees.)

3.
I am warming up soup in Brooklyn,
in Brighton Beach, down by the worn-out ocean.
It's tomato-egg-drop soup from the Chinese take-out,
around the corner, next to the Russian deli
(where the man hums rock 'n' roll, counts change in Yiddish).
Beside me, my daughter watches the TV program.
I watch the tears break out on her face like a rash.
Why is she crying? What can she know of that time?
Me, all my tears are locked up behind my eyes,
rusted like all the words
in the mother language I don't even dream in now.
Me, I don't cry.

Me, I survive and survive.
How I survive! I've outlasted Vilna and Ponar,
the meetings the sewer the forest
the Judenrat and my family
(except for this one, who came later).

My brother stares at us suddenly out of the screen,
out of that photograph I always hated.
He's 20, he's serious, his ears are too big.
I can't look. I turn my back. I lower the flame
under the saucepan, the soup shouldn't burn.
You think it's easy, to concentrate on details?
Details, let me tell you, keep you alive.
Details, I thank God for them.

My daughter looks ugly and old, her face all muddy.
They've got someone else on there now, another story.
I could tell stories too, but I never talked much.

He talked all the time. He scattered his words like salt.
Words, he said, words are important, words can change things.
H sneaked his works in past the guards, he whispered, he shouted
Think of the Jewish people, he said, and he disappeared.
(And the Nazi troop train blew up, and they blamed the Russians.)

She's crying harder, my daughter; sobs choke in her throat like fishbones.
. "Mama," she says, "Mama, why didn't you tell me?"
I say, "What's to tell? Have some soup."

Figure 3.3   Sherry Karver   "Woman in the Window"

Figure 3.4   Chaim Goldberg   "1939-1945"

YOU JUST ASSUME
Lyn Lifshin

the bulge of tulips just
before color,
holding their
rose and blood
in a fist of
green as if to
open would lure
ice back, flatten
the color. A diary
entry wouldn't
do it, even a
video tape that
twisted   curled
into itself like
hair in gleamflame,
a star fish
wrinkling. It
could be Cape
Giradeaux   slow
down the frames
and the beatings
don't connect.
Somewhere frozen
the hand of
knives doesn't
spill blood that
turned new grass
ruby, that could
burst into, clutch
a baby turning to
stone. There was
not any food. Lets
suppose she thought
herself in a film
and plunged in as

if no boots were
real and she
could undress,
feel her mahogany
cuffs slashed from
her and then redo
the scene where
her mother is
shoved, bayonets
in her dress she
can remember the
sheen of into the
blue only gelled
lights turn eerie,
not smell gas

SOSNOWICE, POLAND, SEPTEMBER 1939
Janet Marks

They were young, perhaps married five years,
parents of a three year old girl
and a newborn son. It was early evening,
he had closed his haberdashery shop,
joined his wife and children
for dinner in their building
that housed young families and older ones.
Perhaps they heard the marching feet,
from their windows viewed the black uniforms,
swastika armbands, men with hard faces
marching on their street in time
for women, children and old men
to dash down the basement stairs and hide
before the younger men were lined up, searched,
accused of being Jews.

Women, children, and old men
so paralyzed with fear, they could not breathe
nor make a sound, until the shot
which brought my uncle down, rang out.
The infant whimpered, screwed up its face
to cry. The mother, my aunt,
placed her quivering fingers upon the infant's throat,
squeezed until its breath was gone,
and with a finger to her lips, signaled
the toddler to hush, the baby was asleep.

The shooting ceased, the SS gang
saluted each other, *heiled* Hitler,
marched off, like comic troops, to do their grizzly work
in town. My aunt and her two,
the other women with children, and old men
floundered up the stairs to the charnel house
that was their home.

She laid the infant tenderly
beside its father, and
taking the little girl by the hand
threw themselves upon the corpse of the man
adding their cries to the ghastly din.

Figure 3.5 Judy Herzl "Contemporary Ruins VIII"

Figure 3.6   Deborah Trilling   "My Holy Family"

METAPHOR
/AGE
Paula Naomi Friedman

I don't mean it was easy to escape
at first,
nor borders.
Only, there were the borders;
"over there" those things happened,
only later, here,
in another province.
Many still
—you heard of the most horrible things happening to people
        but across the mountains, mostly—
escaped.

When they rounded us into the square
with their black dogs, bullets
for my brother, my sister and
numbers of the young yet fled
the hundred meters
        to the white birch waving.
And some could still run
away on the march to Vichonitsk,
each scattered flat form
only someone who fell
(here one began
not to feel—
or had one not begun
to feel— the "others"),
forced 60 kilometers through wet snow.

We would hear
the shouts in distant blocks,
and watch through frost-splotched panes
(when we dared glance up)
those selected shuffle,
rarely stride defiant.

Figure 3.7 Deborah Trilling   "Yellow Star"

Past the wires, that summer
typhoid emptied thought but water.
The bottom bunk went for a quota.

We were three who made it through
the nights in the open cars
(few not shot fell
for the woods).
Even in this camp
someone stole a uniform and slipped into a storm
"to tell them—
if they know, they surely
will save you too—"
and the unknown.

Undressing, I am the last survivor
of my memories and everyone I knew,
and while I merge
in the white throng, our bodies sick,
this shaking couple cringing but
putting stunned foot in front of the other,
that grey lady clinging to the ground
until her fingers break,
and the hairless woman who shushes her little one
"It will hurt but don't be scared—
we must pass through the pain to get home"

here,
shoved down this "Way of Heaven"
none escape,
where in the dark
prayers open on unendurable delirium,
the pressure of those before and after on my throat
(our throats),
there must be . . .

Figure 3.8   Barbara Milman   "Auschwitz #10"

IN THE KIBBUTZ LAUNDRY
Elaine Starkman

for Rivke Coop

The number on her arm
appears as I rest in
the dead heat of the noon sun
no longer a nightmare
of story-book horror
that I read in America years ago

She's lived somehow—God knows—
is here now working in the kibbutz laundry
Her hands move in an act of love

When the day ends
and night winds blow
I search out her clear blue eyes
but they reveal nothing

Yet engraved on her arm
lives a page of history
that all the soap
and all the rubbing
can never wash away.

AFTER CLAUDE LANZMAN, SHOAH 1987
Liliane Richman

It was always peaceful
in those deep fir woods
where the sun playfully shot arrows
into slowly shifting shadows,
quiet day and night in the woods not far from my village,
still peaceful after they burned two thousand daily,
after the screams, the barking of dogs,
the hissing of hundreds of bullets
rising to vaulting branches above,
caught there, hanging, trapped in the trees' green canopy.

I thought, then, and now,
don't they deserve axing, these trees,
not stretching their powerful limbs in protest,
not squelching the light twitter of birds?

When all was over
no one watched the mindless river
ferrying kilos of powdered bones downstream.

Figure 3.9 Judy Herzl "I Question"

Figure 3.10   Judy Herzl   "Foot of a Refugee"

ON MURANOWSKA STREET
Myra Sklarew

I have always loved particulars: the angels
bearing a martyr's palm, the way the hair
of the worshippers forms waves or
filaments, the flowers embroidered
on your sleeve. Even my sleep
contains them: the pointed teeth
of mice, a black camera aimed
at my grief. Yet when you ask for the truth
I summon words empty
as air as if I were guarding a sorrow,
encapsulating it that nothing
might come into its vicinity, letting it
ripen. Like the foot of this woman swollen
with callouses, bearing
bits of earth and tar, thorns, remnants
salvaged in it like the map
of the world, pebbles filled with carbon
when the earth was young, fern still
coiled in sandstone. Never mind that he draws
this foot to his lips and kisses the world
that lies imbedded in it, or that beneath
the bellies rolling down to her knees
he sees only the loveliest bones hidden
there, caverns and wetlands he traverses
easily, moving from opening
to opening like a bird metabolizing at a rate
too high to measure. He does not hear
the rifle fire behind her nor the fleeting
sound of hooves. He does not see
twenty men standing on Muranowska
Street, their hands raised in the air.

DREAMING THERESIENSTADT
Susan Terris

No, she told them, gritting teeth, braced.
It's for him. I never eat flesh.

While she watched, he seized
the platter on which lay a severed limb,
skin charred and crisped
like Chinese duck. As his fork pierced,
releasing a sigh of steam, he
tapped a hungry tune on that shin.

Stunned, she recoiled. With a shudder
she swabbed her face
and wet her lips with sour salt.
When he turned, gimlet-eyed, she felt
the ptotic pull of breasts, wished
him still young enough to suckle.

His glance, however, only surveyed,
did not imprint, then reverted
to the feast at hand. Hefting, rending,
shirring, seemingly immune to fumes,
he chewed, raddling
flesh between sharp new teeth.

She felt fingers rotate, tattoo prints
on bone, whorl upon whorl.
Phantom pain pricked as he nibbled,
racked as he gnawed until femur,
patella, tibia, fibula were articulated
only by shreds of cartilage.

Soon a belch, hot and foul, assaulted,
nauseating while he, sated,
extracted splinters from his teeth.
Then, lip-purpled, she mumbled

Kaddish, gripping the table, praying
he would not twitch the cloth,

peer into the darkness beneath,
and learn what, for him, she had yielded.

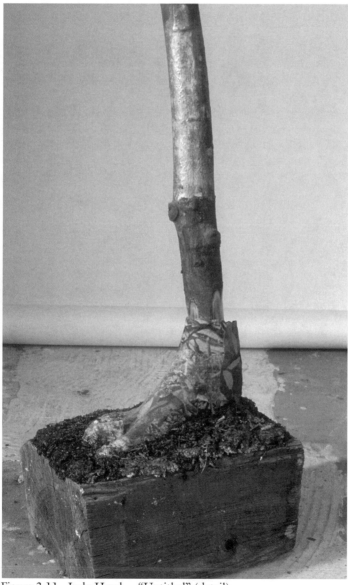

Figure 3.11 Judy Herzl   "Untitled" (detail)

Figure 3.12   Sherry Karver   "Prophetic Vision"

A SCENE FROM THE DEPORTATION
FROM A PHOTOGRAPH OF THE LODZ GHETTO, C1942
Barbara Reisner

"A woman writes her last letter
        before boarding the death train."

People are standing about holding suitcases.
She kneels over a box smoothing out her paper.
The hands are firm with long fingers.
Who has kissed them?
Her hair shines against everything around her.
I want to hold her
        push the hair out of her eyes
                push the train into hell.

She looks like my mother in her youth.
She looks like me in my youth.
She looks like my daughter might look.
A yellow Star of David is sealed on her jacket.

Is she writing: Leaving Lodz.   Going East
Hope this reaches you.   Please don't worry.
I love you.
Was there time to sign her name?
Does she know even nameless I would know her?

The train drives straight through my flesh.
I hold on to her letter.

WARSAW, 1937
Gary Pacernick

The Polish policeman
Towers over the Jewish girl
As he writes out a ticket
Because she has no
license for her bicycle.
People crossing the street
Watch the shapely girl
Who stands holding her bike handles-
Self-contained—looking away
From the policeman
And her fellow citizens
As if for an instant
The future blazes before her eyes.
"Here is your ticket, miss."
She takes it
And slowly peddles away.
People stare at her
Until she disappears
As if they expect to see
Her again, as if she could
Be their child, but they will
Soon forget she ever had a name.

TO CAMILLA, THE LAST JEWISH WOMAN IN MOR
Eva Gross

Shoulders drawn, bending from waist,
wearing an over-washed dress,
eighty and some years old Camilla
shuffles with her bunioned toes,
searching for pennies in the dust.
She's afraid to glance back.
The chafing wind might blow
the ashes into her squinting eyes,
ashes of those she loved
and those who loved her.
Camilla is deaf to the sound of the wind.
In her lives an old tune
her mother sang.
She shakes her head with each step,
"Sorry I'm late, Mama."
She risks a smile that finds no place
on her wrinkled face.
Camilla doesn't look forward
to tomorrow.
Sabbath will come
with so little joy.
The shul is burned to the ground.
Once in a thriving Jewish village,
now no one of her kind greets
her on the street.
What's there to see
at the bend of the road?
The days pass without
her permission.
Camilla reaches her home,
kisses the holy scroll
on the doorpost
as there is no one
left to be kissed.

Figure 3.13   Barbara Milman   "Conflagration"

SUPPER
Rochelle Natt

Unbearable, she thinks, the clacking
of fork tines against china and teeth.
Even the bow slide
of speared meat is discordant.

Spoons are merciful
in the silence of scooping cantaloupe
from the grainy rind, wetted and dark
as moss and bracken.

She does not flinch
at the whip crack of hunger
History demands she eat black bread,
matchstick fingers picking, picking.

A crust tucked in her sleeve
near the backstitched seam of folded money.
Someone can be paid to look away
as she passes through the gate.

Why is she the only one here at the table
whose nostrils fill with singed air?
Why are her eyes
plugged into sockets of night?

Soon she'll be whittled down
to bone and soul.
There will be no chewing, no clink
of glass or silverware to jar her.

Her body will leave itself,
become a spiderweb
the living disturb
as they pass through darkness.

THE REFUGEE
Barbara Unger

Tides of World War Two
begin to turn
as I jump rope
and mother seeks
lebensraum in the West Bronx
with the Amalgamated unionists.

We trek through Tante Bertha's rooms
redolent with floor polish and prosperity
and she tells of her escape from Hitler,

Diamonds sewn into sleeves
of her woolen *shmates*
as she edged her way
from Prague's Jewish Quarter
to Japanese-occupied Shanghai,

Buying silence and safe passage
with the rubies of redemption
sewn inside the shoulders
of her gabardine suits,

Her life hanging
in the balance
in the red-glow dark
of her cavernous
Chinese closets.

UNTIL THE DAY BREATHE
Barbara Reisner

Black water   night tree
long rooted and thin reaching
by frail stretches into
the world   Shulamit

in Auschwitz   the sun
has scorned her   she speaks:
When a body lies in its own
excrement uses the same bowl
for eating and shitting   and
there is no water   you can lose
your will to live

Shulamit walks along the
perimeter of the brain   dark
brain ribbon of face   sees
the millions fall along
the road   mud deep
in the breach

She hears god bang a tin
cup against the night
tree   hears him cry out
faces   faces in my cup
they offer up the faces
and she has her own
bowl tied around her
waist

she lies under a mattress
on top lies a dead woman
Shulamit eats her bread and
wears her shoes

She is young and comely
and thinks of her lover
swimming in the dark
water   his own face is
neither water nor flesh
but a fleeting numinous
breath   he

calls her water gypsy   she

wanders through smoke and
bone exhuming sustenance
from the dead There
is no water

Shulamit is black with grief
the sun has scorned her
Her lover swims in the dark
water and cannot recognize
the day from night he comes
to her as shadow
she has eaten the bread of
the dead   she

pours his shadow into
her bowl it runs like a
gazelle upon the mountains of
spice   and she empties
it upon her mouth

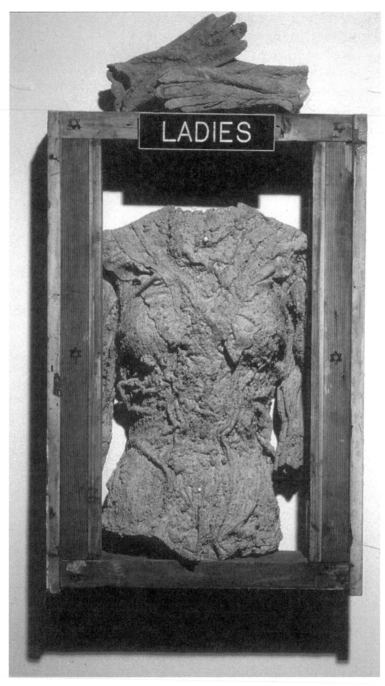

Figure 3.14 Deborah Trilling *"Schmuckstück/Schmeckstück"* ("Garbage/Jewel")

SOMEWHERE IN POLAND . . .
SURVIVOR'S LAMENT
Heidemarie Pilc

Lost in an alien forest
I pray at my people's tomb,
lazy beams of sunlight
drift through autumn leaves
vanish
beneath darkening skies.

My parents and my siblings
fifty-two years ago
murdered
by thugs in uniform
reappear
in millions of heartaches
chiseled into a memorial of stone,
towering monument of a nation's conscience.
Reminder of the charred remains
of my people's fatal years.

I weep at my people's grave
want them as desperately
as the dark beneath the ground
wants light,
want to dig under the stone,
stir their ashes alive, hear the earth speak them—
so still these fifty-two years—
turn their sighs and moans
into shouts of hallelujah.

Want you back brothers and sisters,
mother and father
to be your child again.

People of the earth now,
long delivered from their tormentors,
one with the ancient walls,

dust of shtetl streets,
lying in whispers
of Kaddish
and candlelight

Figure 3.15   Barbara Milman   "Shtetl Nostalgia" (detail)

A LITTLE BEETHOVEN IN THE BACKGROUND
Barbara Reisner

for Eva Lesavoy

"The Lord waits to be gracious to you."
Isaiah 30:16

Germany, 1945. A house
crowded with women
about to be set on fire.
Dark-haired Eva runs outside
and digs in the cold ground.

She prays for the soldier
who points his rifle at her.
—*Eli. Eli.* God, why hast Thou forsaken me?
He orders her to sing the *Ave Maria.*
She hears a shot and falls down.

The German, also on the ground,
is killed by a Russian and an American
who hear her singing.
The American newspapers say
she saved a thousand women from burning.

On this second night
of Rosh Hashanah
she holds up the honey-dipped apple,
she invites the Lord's graciousness.
She tells of Moses
who, needing a miracle,
struck the rock in the desert.

Now Eva is in a field
and a young soldier strikes women
in the head. They will be shot
if they talk to the guards,
but Eva remembers the impatience
of Moses and the breaking of stone.

She walks toward the guard
as he eats his lunch.
—How awful for you to eat here
in this miserable field;
how much happier for you at home
with your family, a little Beethoven
in the background.

He stands up and points to her.
Instead of shooting he gives
her a piece of bread and
doesn't hit the women.

Twenty years later Eva
rides into Jerusalem.
—I and not Moses?

Her face, carved from the slain
of the earth, decomposes slowly,
like a millennium thrust
with the will of God.

Gone into the night
her benedictions, watchful,
unseal the unmarked names

from THE TESTING OF HANNA SENESH
Ruth Whitman

23

I remember the two Polish women
who came to Palestine
escaped from a death camp
and the news they brought:

Some did not believe,
but I knew:

now I follow a path
back to the fiery center

to rescue a live ember

16

I am already the widow of my life:

I chose a way separate
but paved with light,

a promise that I would be
a gift accepted,

that the world and I
would join rejoicing:

but now I am
married to solitude,

sister of death,
a gift that went astray

35

There is a fire in me:
it must not go to waste.

Sitting in the snow,
I fan it with my breath.

I cup it with my hands:
it must not be lost.

I am the fire.
I am the moth.

37

Perhaps I'm not iron.

At first I felt nothing could bend me,
but now I'm not so sure.
They laughed at me when I said I was shot down.
They know I've been with the partisans.

They keep beating the palms of my hands,
the soles of my feet.
They keep asking for the transmitter code.

I'm not so sure I can stand more beatings.
The detective twists my arm,
telling me I am now state property.
I say I am no one's property.

38

Blessed is the match that burns and kindles fire,
blessed is the fire that burns in the secret heart,
Blessed are the hearts that know how to stop with honor...
blessed is the match that burns and kindles fire.

FIRST THOUGHTS:
ON LIBERATION DAY FROM CONCENTRATION CAMP
Annette Harchik

I will leave my prison,
climb down from filthy bunks
tiered six layers high,
and escape the drone of commands,
work details, and whippings,

to give free reign
to my breath, and arms,
and sex,
and dance my steps of ecstasy
however slowly.

I will crawl out
from the corners
of this creviceless space
where my body has huddled
for countless days,
and stumble into the sunlight.

I who have dared to live to this day
Now dare to leave the darkness of this place.

Figure 3.16 Wolf Kahn "Sharing Survivors"

I DREAMED HIM HOMEWARD
Yala Korwin

for E.K., whose brother went down with Struma

"The small steamer Struma, with 750 Jewish refugees from Rumania and Bulgaria aboard, was blown to pieces in the Black Sea about five miles north of the Bosphorus, apparently by a stray mine…There have been no reports of survivors."
　　　　　The New York Times, Feb. 25, 1942

He came to say good-bye:
"My sheepskin cap fooled them,
they took me for their own.
The Iron Guard let me pass.
The others? From Prayer House
to slaughterhouse. Quartered. Hung.
One ship got through to Palestine.
There is hope. I'll go."

I dreamed him only from the knees down,
but knew it was my brother.
These elongated bones of youth,
so full of vigor,
yet wrapped in rotting flesh,
treaded the black-green water.

I was the raging sea.
It was my body that yielded
to spidery rolling of his limbs.
Walk, walk my brother,
I'll guide you where
you want to go! My voice was
a rumbling of waves.

A day after the dream,
a postcard, his hand: "We are
cooped here forever. No toilets.
Most are sick. The boat unseaworthy,

but the Turks wouldn't let us land."
Mother pressed the letter
to trembling lips:
"Thank God. He lives."

Walk, walk my brother
Where you want to go.
No entry papers needed
anymore.

from *THE TESTING OF HANNA SENESH, #6*
Ruth Whitman

The death ships. The *Struma*.
It lay in the harbor at Istanbul
Without food or coal.

Don't let it land,
said the Ambassador.

Jews are enemy aliens,
said the British.
Tow them out to the Black Sea,
send them to Crete, Mauritius,
to Rumania, Germany, Jamaica,
but don't let them come to Palestine.

That was December 1941.

Safe in my kibbutz at Sdot Yam
(meadows of the sea),
              I looked
at the peacock-blue Mediterranean
and cried, let them come,
we have room.

No, said Lord Moyne,
if one ship comes
they'll all want to come.

Let the children come.

Children?
What will we do with children?

The hold was airless.
Sickness, filth,
layers of excrement, vomit.

The ship could not sail.
The ship could not stay.
No land would take them.

In February the ship exploded
outside the harbor in Istanbul.
eight hundred lives flew up,
their rags, arms, legs, hopes,
falling like rain.

One was saved.
He was allowed to enter
Palestine.

Figure 3.17   Chaim Goldberg   "The Black Sun"

WARSAW, 1946
Barbara Reisner

"In the day he that escapeth shall come unto thee, and cause thee to hear it." (Ezek. 24:26-27)

After the war
an old Jew whose
face was dissolving into
a lost word
had been refused a death.
He sat outside the shred
of a building where he used
to live.   They had made him
become a newspaper. They said   It's you
we're telling whom we've killed and who's
left to live.
People came to him and asked   What
happened to Bayla   to Anna   to Shrul
to Sarah   to Malka   and he would tell
them   Shrul died in Auschwitz
Malka was shot in the woods   they let
Bayla live   Sarah keeps looking for her
children   Anna died in the ghetto of hunger

The old man could no longer say
I was Nate the apple peddler I am
tired   He could no longer say
I

DYING INSTRUCTIONS
David Gershator

from and for Abba

Abba
father
teacher
rabbi
without answers
comes back often
and kids around
he leaves me with a smile
sometimes I wake up laughing
but sometimes he's dead serious
telling me to die in my sleep
if I have a choice
the day he died in his sleep
in his own bed
was one of the best
he confides
better to die not knowing
than be born not knowing
it's everything in between
all the disappeared
that Hitler hung
around your neck
all that knowing
and not knowing
that makes closing your eyes
forever
a gift from some god
the same god, perhaps,
who closes his eyes
to everything

Figure 3.18 Sherry Karver   "Souvenirs"

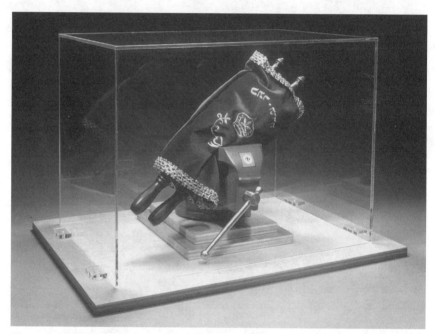

Figure 3.19   Harold Lewis   "The Final Solution"

ANGEL: 178TH STREET, NEW YORK CITY
Stewart Florsheim

Every morning on 178th Street he rummaged
through the trash for his daily paper.
I watched him from across the street,
the cantor who inspired tears
when he taught me the haftorah
for my Bar Mitzvah. Sunday afternoons,
I went to his third-floor apartment
that had the odor of chicken soup
and feather beds that had not been aired.
I walked down his long dark corridor
and sat with him at the dining room table.
He opened the haftorah for the book of *Genesis*
and I began to read my portion, *Toldoth Yitzhak*.
You have to do better, he would say,
I want your parents to be so proud of you.
After the lesson he unrolled a lace tablecloth
over the table then walked around it,
carefully unraveling each fringe:
My wife brought this back from Germany.

With the same hands he searched
through the broken Coke bottles, used Kleenexes.
He picked up one or two papers
till he found the one he wanted,
that day's *Daily News*. Perhaps
it was his way of honoring the past,
back in Germany, once it became Judenrein
and he had no money or dignity,
save for his faith in God that would
inspire him to sing like an angel.

Figure 3.20   Leah Korican   "Gifts from the Air"

THE BIRD NAMED ISIDORE
Evelyn Posamentier

in memory of my father, Ernest Posamentier

there is a story about a hummingbird named Isidore.
In the story, also, is the man who owns him.
This is a children's story but adults, too, secretly
yearn for it.
The man & the bird isidore are seen against
the backdrop of a faraway city. In the city there is a palace.
The palace appears
in each illustration. Silent symphonies are heard in blue orchestration
whenever the palace rises in the pink & weightless mind
of the reader.
The bird is white as a spot
of happiness in a fairy tale.
The bird named isidore watches from his window
as the man & his friends ride the ferris wheel.
& the air hums with dreams.
Because one of the pages is missing
& next we see the man in a dark factory
groping through a life in a language he doesn't
understand, we fear
that something terrible has happened.
Sadly the pages turn. Over the years, love & light
dim to a steady drone.
But sometimes
in a bright yellow moment
of a Sunday morning when the stores are closed
the bird stirs the wings in the man's mind, its breeze
sets slowly in motion the ferris wheel, the ferris wheel.
He mentions, half whispering, to his children
the story about the bird named isidore so near
to the touch. One of the children waits
for more stories
but there are none:
the man has no past.
only this one white spot.
The child is too frightened to ask:
& *what else happened?*

Figure 3.21   Irv Wieder   "Adam & Eve"

THE ARMOIRE
Ruth Marmorstein

The Goddamn thing stood where the bed should have been. Bigger than he remembered, it loomed like a ghastly specter from hell come to haunt him. How could he have ever let her buy it?

The bile rose in his throat as he strode angrily across the room and set his suitcase on the floor—she followed, her voice still chirping on about cleaning and polishing it all day.

He watched her walk over and lovingly touch it, "The movers said there's not a nail in it—you know, honey, they only deliver antiques and they said they've never, ever, seen anything like it before."

"Get it out of here."

The bewildered angry look, the question, half-formed on her lips were replaced with an expression of such terrible sadness that he ran after her as she turned to leave the room.

His touch, meant to comfort, was rough when she tried to pull away. He bent to catch her words. "I thought you liked it. Why did you give me the money to have it delivered on our anniversary?"

"Because I wanted to make you happy." There was no response to his kiss.

He left the next morning and was on the road for two days checking the landscaping of the construction sites. When he returned the top piece with carved roses had been removed and stood on her dresser. It was a foot high.

How the hell did she lift that heavy piece down? She thinks without the fuckin' roses it looks better. "It still looks like hell. I said get it out of here."

"Honey, I tried—I called Alice to help, but we could only push it halfway across the room—we couldn't push it any farther so we just put it back—but don't worry, I'll get it out of here. I'll put an ad in the paper Thursday. Can it stay here until I sell it?"

He looked at her pleading face. Why in the hell was she so nice? Why didn't she scream, we looked at it through the window. You came home and measured. You said I could have it. She didn't scream because that wasn't her style.

He watched her mother push her around before they were married and it had upset him. He hated people who inflicted their will on others. He had taken enough of that. Never again would anyone tell him what to do.

"I bought it for you honey,—for your shirts and sweaters." She opened the doors and he saw his shirts and sweaters folded neatly on the shelves. On the other side hung his suits, below them his shoes were carefully arranged.

"We thought you'd like it better without the top piece" she raised her hands helplessly, "maybe it was too feminine with the roses—I don't know why you don't . . ." her voice trailed off and she shrugged, and again lifted her hands in a helpless gesture. He wanted to reach out and touch her, wipe away that anguished look. What was he doing to her anyway?

The phone rang. He knew it would be her best friend Alice. She couldn't take a crap without asking Alice.

"He still hates it. How should I know. No, I have to get rid of it—maybe it reminds him of something."

He sat on the edge of the bed and stared at it. They could have hurt themselves trying to move it. Damn thing must weigh a ton. He hadn't remembered it well. Tucked in amongst the other wooden pieces in the back of the cluttered antique shop, it hadn't seemed so formidable. But now, standing alone, it commanded the entire room. He should have gone in and looked at it. The next day she had suggested, but he had said no—if she liked it that was all that mattered. She could have anything she wanted on their tenth anniversary.

It no longer held his clothes when he returned from work the next evening. One door stood ajar, the inside mirror reflecting its emptiness. He walked to the window, unable to hold back the flood of memories any longer.

His mother's had been pink, heavily carved. Maybe Venetian or French in design. He remembered as a small child lying in his parents' bed; nestled amongst the down pillows and quilts—he would watch her take clothes from it. He could still see her reflected in the inside mirrored doors, see her laughing face as she turned her body so that their eyes met.

So many years had passed that when he tried to make a composite of her features he was unable to, he could remember neither the color of her eyes nor the shape of her face, whether her lips had been thin or fleshy like his own or exactly what color her hair had been. He thought she had been small, but he wasn't even really sure of that, painful as it had been, he had gradually come to the realization that memory was a luxury he could ill afford.

But he could still see her eyes reflected in the mirrored doors. He could still see *their* devil faces laughing under the death's head. . . *their* boots on the highly polished wooden floor as they slashed and threw her clothes to the floor. He could still feel them tearing him from her arms, beating him away, turning that beautiful laughing face into the frozen mask of horror it had become the last time he saw her.

It was the image that awoke him again and again, wrenching him from a tormented sleep only to realize it was a nightmare he could do no more about now than he could as a boy of fifteen. He wanted to kill *them*. He wanted to smash those devil faces until there was nothing to smash, until they were only a bloody pulp, until they stopped laughing.

He found himself kicking it again and again, pounding it until he heard her voice and looked down to see his knuckles raw and bloodied. He turned to see her standing in the doorway. "I don't want anything bigger than I am in this room."

"Don't upset yourself. I've already put an ad in the paper. I know I'll sell it. It's so beautiful I shouldn't have any trouble—the woman said it's over 150 years old—"

"You believe anything anyone tells you. I'm going to sleep for an hour. I'm exhausted."

He listened for her singing as she did the dishes and it dawned on him that he hadn't heard it for some time. Serves her right—she believes anything—like his father—they had been told they were going to be *resettled in the east.* . .

All Thursday morning he thought about it. He knew she had always wanted one, ever since she was a little girl and she played hide-and-seek in one her aunt had owned.

He came home from the office at noon with severe cramps. She was alarmed because he never took time off and wanted to call the doctor. He looked at her anxious face and wanted to say something to reassure her, but instead he snapped that he wanted to be left alone.

Why couldn't he just tell her that he loved her and that he really wanted her to have it, but it was taking on a life of its own, that it was forcing him to think about things that he didn't want to remember.

He lay down on their bed. He wanted to sleep, but his body fought to stay awake—he couldn't afford to sleep . . . couldn't afford to lower his defenses or they would take him away as they had taken his father . . . only four months before liberation . . . why hadn't he been able to hold on just a little longer?

The memories, three dimensional with color and sound track rolled on, his mother laughing and then the taste of blood in his mouth as the rifle butt smashed again and again, and above it all, the sound of her screaming.

With the scream still ringing in his ears he sat up as she tiptoed into the room. "Honey, someone's coming to see it. Lie down in one of the kids' rooms."

His insides twisted. "Don't sell it. Get someone to move it—put it in the back of the house—anywhere, just so I don't have to look at it."

The following evening his new partner came to the house for dinner. Alex had once been in the family's antique business; he admired the beautiful old pieces she had collected throughout the fifty year old house.

When they got to the master bedroom Alex walked up to the wardrobe and began caressing it. "My God, do know what you have here?"

She nodded. "Yes, the woman I bought it from told me it's at least 150 years old."

"It might be older than that." He heard the excitement in Alex's voice. "This is Caucasian "Do you see these panels? The burled wood was perfectly matched." Alex extended his arm, "the small inserts up here, they're ebony you know."

Alex walked over to the dresser and touched the top piece. "Look at the artistry of this carving. Sometimes you find a signature or initials if it was done by an outstanding craftsman. It would pay for you to look. This is a collector's item—a museum piece."

"It's not ours anymore. I sold it."

"Sold it? Why?"

"Oh, I don't know," she shrugged, "it's awfully big."

"Big? This room is enormous," Alex said. "You've got 10 foot ceilings."

He pulled her to him in the dark. "Don't sell it."

"Honey, forget it. It's sold."

"Did she pay you?"

"No. I told her to give me the money when it's picked up Saturday."

"Then it's not sold."

"Of course it is. I gave her my word . . ."

"Tell her your husband will divorce you if you sell it."

He felt her stiffen. He fell asleep holding her.

When he returned from work on Saturday it was on the truck. The movers were carefully covering it. Movers that handle only antiques she had told him.

He took the stairs two at a time, then doubled over with pain when he saw her. Weeping, she was dragging the bed across the floor and sobbing as if her heart would break. When he reached her she clung to him. He stood kissing her tears away. Next to his side of the bed she had placed a bouquet of roses from the garden.

LOUIE THE TAILOR
Gary Pacernick

While I stuffed wrapping paper
Into boxes, Louie the tailor
Worked upstairs in the loft
At Jack's Haberdashery.
A tiny man with big blue
Watery eyes and a high-pitched
Heavily accented voice,
He stood behind the huge iron.
Steam rose to the ceiling
As Louie pressed out the wrinkles
In newly purchased garments.
The arm of the iron rose and fell
In a staccato beat, hissing
With heat. Just as hot to me
Was the nude Marilyn Monroe
Calendar pinned to the cracked wall
Behind Louie, who never seemed to notice it.
Louie, the proud husband and father,
Was happy to be pressing clothes
Upstairs in the steamy loft
At Jack's Haberdashery
Far, far from the ovens of Auschwitz.

Figure 3.22   Lisa Kokin   "Remembrance"

Figure 3.23   Chaim Goldberg   "Message 1943"

IF WHEN YOU HEAR ME
Seymour Mayne

If when you hear me
you think it is prayer
take it as prayer

My fingers will be
cupping the last food—
large beans nourishing
without the slaughterer's hand
to bless them

You will be stronger then
Two will stand at my side
and bid me follow—
each in his direction
wanting my blood and presence

In the past and future
know me as prayer
dance of your twin lips

Hear me and I am heard
Ears rip open with a flutter
like books And pages of steel
sprout in the deep silences
before mass slaughter

Figure 3.24   Wolf Kahn   "The Soldier and the Survivor"

NOT ONLY IN THE SIX-DAY WAR
Charles Fishman

Not only in the Six-Day War
but in the locked ghettoes
there were heroes,
in the selections, the cattle trains,
the forced marches, even under torture,
as the gas embraced them, in smoke
billowing, in the blood ditches,
even in the death sleep after liberation,
the DP camps, frail ships, desert
massacres, even in hospitals and orchards,
kibbutz nurseries, zealots' outposts,
even in the day-to-day dream of remembering
what was ours, over thousands of years,
in this moment when I remind you,
my sisters and brothers, how courageous
we have been, how bravely
we have arrived at this hour.

Figure 4.1   Cynthia Moskowitz Brody   "Girl Alone/House Alone"

IV.

Inheritance

COUNTING BACKWARDS (1973)
Evelyn Posamentier

you & your sisters said I had the head of a thirty year old
at 6, I believed you, you were my mother,
& an orthodox jew doesn't lie; you said this
& I heard you, thru my tears as you
dragged me to the synagogue-
the unwanted dress squeezed tighter than a boa.

At 13, when my suicide face hung plain as the ironed
shirts that you folded away so neatly,
I asked
& you turned away,
I cried
& you snapped on the radio—
we always ate lunch quietly.

At 16, when I exposed the nightly horror films that entered my life
without knocking, you said that I
thought too much, was influenced by the wrong crowd
didn't really have much to complain about considering
I didn't come from a broken home (or anything like that)

& besides, what did I think the young girls
did in dachau?

AUSCHWITZ—SECOND GENERATION
Cynthia Moskowitz Brody

> to my mother, Hermina Moskowitz,
> who tries so hard to live in the present.

I can recall it now
that sickened   sinking
weight within me
when she spoke of
        that time in her life
and she'd almost smile as if to
soothe me   as if to say
It's only a movie
except it wasn't
and it's sleeping in her somewhere
and used to scream out
in my dreams

They shaved her head of course
something about lice or dirt
among so many
and
they
lined
up
naked
daily
and he'd smile at her
that man whose *game*
it was to choose
the timber for the day
So she could live for awhile
not like her sisters
and their children who went
wide eyed
        and were gone

Now she'll squeeze her bulging middle
and laugh that even then
she had this extra flesh
and how it kept her from the ovens

She says
they smelled it
in the air
the smell
of those they loved
but she wouldn't believe it   and she worked
leaving fear and hope
among her other belongings
in the heap
And though they didn't brand her skin
she wears her numbers
in her eyes

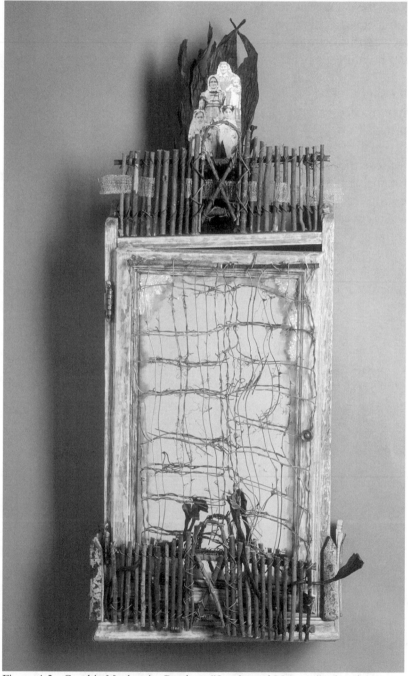

Figure 4.2 Cynthia Moskowitz Brody   "Smoke and Memory" (closed)

Figure 4.3   Cynthia Moskowitz Brody   "Smoke and Memory" (open)

BELATED *KADDISH**
Cynthia Moskowitz Brody

in memory of those lost, and those who tried to save them.

Photographs and stone
from another time and place,
embedded deep in primal parts
we cannot see
but know too well,
remind us of the ones
we would have loved
had the world chosen to see.

Now, with photographs and stone
I put to rest
the sad-eyed souls
who haunt me still
who find their way onto my canvas
their final resting place.

I give them the gift of stones
to mark their time spent
on this earth.
A simple gift
forbidden in their own time
when their songs and dances,
words and thoughts, were
insignificant   dangerous
to people who needed them
to disappear
and take all the evils
with them to their
unmarked secret graves.

Fifty years have passed
and yet they will not be still
They call out from the dust,
grow into the branches of
the trees with which they mingle,

sing their ancient songs
across the oceans
and find their way
to my outstretched hand
stroking the melody in colors
green and gold,

slipping from my veins
onto this memorial piece

The stone has been a gift to me
from one with different songs.
His people from the other side
would have been allowed to live,
easily
except for their choice
to harbor those
they would not abhor,
to live a Christian life.
And in the end
gave their lives
for what that meant to them.
Three generations   lost in a moment
for having a conscience.
Sought out by those who did not.

And so we are both marked
though the graves are not,
and he is pleased to add
his voice to this testimonial.
We both carry the torch
to be passed down
to our children
and their children
so that they will learn
the true meaning of
hero.

Kaddish is the Hebrew prayer for the dead.

Figure 4.4   Cynthia Moskowitz Brody
"Six Million Voices Call to Me 'Never Forget' "

HAUNTED KISSES
Cynthia Moskowitz Brody

We
who live in
the black and white images of
a vanished world
        can get lost in the full color ripeness
        of a present moment

We
whose mothers lived in Hell
their shorn heads filled with
memories of safer times
to keep them warm
        have found our way to one another

The ink that
by some miracle bypassed
their helpless arms
        has pierced the numbered tattoos into
        our own exploding hearts
        which turn toward ink again
        for the mercy of words

You say you don't want to
know me
just to love my body
        -just-
but this is what you
need to know
That this soft flesh
this curve of finger
shallow well of throat
is the housing of my soul
and has wiped too many
trampling feet

Come in rather
through smaller portals
a little at a time so I can see
who you are
and not only who
I reflect
and I can hear
not only your panting
but your held breath

We
whose beginnings
could have been
our end
whose seeds were planted
in the blackest soil
were nourished by the ashes
of those we never knew

And in our bones live
shining threads and gallows ropes
woven tightly pulling us toward
the next survival
A coming together such as this is not
a moan in the night   it is a private entrance
a sacred place
and I have always known
the password

Figure 4.5 Cynthia Moskowitz Brody
"And We Never Even Know We Have the Key"

MY WEEPING WILLOW
Laura Zusman (written when she was 12 years old)

My bloody back I cannot feel
leaning against the weeping willow
Strong
heavy
thick tangles of branches hide me
from their view.
From their screaming,
cold
blurry view
of the world around them.
My walnut eyes
wide with fear
shift to my bony hands
lying lifeless in my lap.
Those hands cracked and bruised
that once touched such a petite form of life
that they seized and carried off
Away from me, from Mama
The winds cry into my ears
forcing the leaves of the weeping willow onto my pale cheeks
The smooth tiny leaves
unaware of the horror around them.
I carefully caress a leaf in my ugly hands
I imagine it is Mama
hiding me from them
I see Daddy in the leaves
Each leaf is one of us
protecting me from Them.
My weeping willow's branches seem to sag around me.
Mama and Daddy were strong.
They are in my weeping willow.
My weeping willow is of us.
Am I somewhere in my weeping willow?
Am I like Mama and Daddy?
Mama didn't hide.

I close my eyes.
My weeping willow sags lower around me,
just like my hopes
The tree prays
and I join in
Praying to God.

Figure 4.6   Cynthia Moskowitz Brody   "Family Tree"

Figure 4.7   Cynthia Moskowitz Brody   "Only in Dreams"

STONES
Elizabeth Rosner

three hundred years ago
or yesterday
I walked on the smooth stones
of a riverbed
grief flowing quietly alongside me and
birds calling to one another
from high treetops above
my head where I couldn't
see anything

>   this is what I need you to understand
>   that the grief is part of this scene
>   it belongs here
>   and every stone is its own piece
>   the sharp-edged ones
>   the cracked and imperfect ones
>   those shaped like fists or eggs or bones
>   they speak in the language of the river

I wanted to go naked
into the cold clear water
rinse away every trace
of every moment except
this one but
I didn't

I sat on the sand at the
edge of the water and
listened to every story
over and over
learning again that the truth
follows a path it knows
by heart

BIRTHRIGHT
Elizabeth Rosner

there are no portraits
of ancestors
hanging on my walls
no heirlooms in velvet-lined boxes
my legacy is in my bones
in the grief I wear beneath my skin
a secret that never
goes away but is passed
through the coded messages
of blood and that other
substance we have no name for

Figure 4.8 Cynthia Moskowitz Brody "Devotion to God"

CAFÉ MIT SCHLAG
Jacqueline Fishman

The coffee room in Vienna.
Afternoon Napoleons in the city of Maria Theresia.
Steam-frosted cups of espresso topped with clouds of sweet
    whipped cream.
Mocha and cinnamon drift on the quiet air.
In a sleek glass vase on each table, a thorned rose.

We have come to retrace the landscape of chaos.
Flight. Vienna to Prague.
Deportation. Theresienstadt.
End of the line. Birkenau
    To Block 3 Eichmann's Auschwitz
    from 22 Silbergasse in Klimt's Vienna.

Mother-knot.
Inlaid lines cross the mahogany table,
echoing the intricate entanglements
fixing me to the storyteller opposite, their embedded fibers braided
into an invisible umbilical cord binding
me to my mother forever.

Mother-rot.
Amid the clinking of coffee spoons rises the ghost of my grandmother.
A story never heard.
Abandonment.
My grandmother embraces her lover's fate rather than her own
    child's.
A young girl forsaken in the whirlwind.

Mother-not.
There are broken lines in this matriarchy.
I have studied images of mothers who walked knowingly into the gas
    with their children,
women who could no longer breathe when they saw their own

Figure 4.9   Chandra Garsson   "Doublethink"

children
    flung discus-like across the sky.
But not this mother.
This mother simply said
good-bye.

My mother wonders at my passion for my daughter.
An eye askance, she is slightly amused.
Of course.
She hears the wailing mother whose infant was ripped from her breast
She sees the child drop dead from hunger.
She screams into the abyss of not being chosen.

How dare I have this joy?

WHAT'S REALLY TRUE
Beth Aviv Greenbaum

In a parking garage in Birmingham
on a day so hot the boy sought shade,
a white man ordered "Lie on the ground
or I'll shoot," and he pressed his rifle's butt

into his shoulder and aimed
at the boy he believed
was stealing his other car,
a black Jaguar. Suburban racism,

the papers said. Turns out
the white man's a child
of holocaust survivors, he's married,
has a son, pays his dues

to the ADL and ACLU.
By day he's a neurosurgeon—severs
bad flesh from good, then scrubs his hands
and sterilizes his greens.

By night he turns in his wife's arms
to dream again—black boots,
raised rifles, running, being chased,
groveling for grace.

"Don't you hear the bombers,
the tanks?" "You're dreaming,"
she whispers, "You hear traffic
on Woodward, the three a.m. train."

Even with his arms around his wife in their bed
every fence is electric, every kid a thief,
every cement floor a place to press his cheek
to feel the gravelly cold in all the heat.

MEYER TSITS AND THE CHILDREN
Jason Sommer

In the gone world of Roman Vishniac's book
of photographs of Jewish Eastern Europe,
which we sit down to look over,
my father recognizes for certain only
the village idiot of a Munkács neighborhood,
Meyer "Tsits," whom they used to tease:
"Your mother has breasts,"
the children would say as they passed,
and frothing with rage he would give chase
some years before breasts and Meyer were ash.

In the picture, though, Meyer is
contentedly on his way to a meal at the home
of the prosperous burgher who walks beside him
wielding a cane and wearing a *shtreimel*.
(My father thinks the fur hat means it must be *Shabbos*.)
Meyer's benefactor protects the sable tails
from the drizzle with a draped handkerchief
and performing his mitzvah, taking
an unfortunate home to dinner,
he looks more foolish than the fool.

Even in the still one can tell how Meyer moves
on rain-glossed Boco Corsi,
hands tucked into opposite sleeves
making a muff, shuffling the spanceled
steps of a Chinese woman
when Vishniac sights him,
transfers his photographer's gaze down through
the viewfinder of the hidden reflex camera
held at his solar plexus
and out through the lens that peers through
the gap in his overcoat.
In the direction of the background,
straight back until the stacks of firewood,

up stairs behind wrought iron,
through the tiled entry,
rooms burst with Rabinovitz's court
where Hassidim argue passionately
over matters of indifference
to those outside their picture
of the world to come, the Messiah,
and the immortality of the soul.

Out of the book open on a table
in the dining room of this house,
I extend the scale of the photograph
into the world—
and my father's cellar rooms
in 1937 would be somewhere
in the schoolyard of this suburban
New York neighborhood.
But my father would not yet have been there.
Even at the late hour of the photograph,
age fifteen, he welded in Fisher's bike shop
on Kertvarosh, which crosses a few blocks
from where Meyer walks,
and my grandmother Yitta Feiga
still launders clothes in someone's basement.

Vishniac clicks his shutter.
Meyer is caught especially unaware,
after and before—no children near to show him
stripped to his oedipal machinery,
though here in this moment, as in his rage
or his final agony, he was incapable of other modes than candor.

Meyer himself would have survived no selection.
He would have been among the first,
as in 1940 they practiced Holocaust
on his sort just to get the knack.
The picture has been hidden, captured,
liberated, restored while other negatives perished
in the journey from their moments.

My father, who has come through much to get here,
prepares to turn the page.
His own escape and liberation
may not be on his mind now.
There are so many losses and Meyer is little to him,
so few survivals and a picture something but not enough.
The dearest faces to him from then
are faces not in this book,
faces of which there are no extant images
outside of memory.

Meyer Tsits and the children
may not signify to him that before the astounding
cruelties are the ordinary ones,
which have been restored to us at least—
the cruelties of sons and fathers,
cruelties which may be partially redeemed
by forgiveness, and therefore for which
forgiveness is seldom sought,
cruelties not on a street which leads to streets
which lead to the camps
where Meyer still and always in his first
childhood, in his first love and jealousy,
was first for the gas.

I delay with questions the turning of the page.
What does the sign behind them—Mydlow—mean? How old was
Meyer?
And it comes to me suddenly that I want
my father to ask forgiveness of Meyer Tsits
for peasant amusements,
laughing the blank laugh
at those one thinks one never will become,
and that I must ask, too, for having made
some part of his life and death
into coin, capital for speculation.
And to ask forgiveness of Meyer Tsits is to
imagine him restored to faculties
he may never have had,

and to believe for a photographic instant
in the immortality of the soul.

Figure 4.10   Harley Gaber   "Die Plage" (Section 2)

THE GOLD WATCH
Beth Aviv Greenbaum
for Rifka

You gave to me a watch
with a band of woven gold
when I gave birth

to your first grandchild,
child of a child of a child
of Auschwitz. "She is a gift

for my mother," your son said
as he held her bloody, unwashed
in the fluorescent light of Sinai Hospital.
"She is the proof," he said,
"the chain was not broken,
Hitler did not prevail."

And he handed me our daughter
to nurse. We named her Sari,
after your sister. Years later,

we divorced, split Sari between us,
and at the estate sale I sold that watch
for far less that it was worth.

A STAB
Sari Aviv (written Spring, 1994 when she was 14 years old)

We expected to hear
a friendly message
on the answering machine.
"Dead you Jews," a boy's voice hissed
in a pseudo German accent.
My body began shaking violently,
like a revved up engine.
My head grew too heavy for my neck.
Salt water screamed
from my opened eyes.
I saw my grandmother
sleeping on a plywood bunk,
water dripping all night
on her back.
How she wanted to die.
I saw my great grandparents sent
to the line on the right.
I saw smoke and ashes in the air.

My friends tried
to comfort me.
They still did not know.

OUT OF TIME AND PLACE
David Gershator

Looking back over my shoulder
I see an old couple
They beckon to me
as if I know them
as if they know me . . .
They've been shadowing me
for a long long time
They're self effacing and silent
yet somehow we know each other

I never saw them before
but I sense who they are
never knew what they looked like
not a single photo . . .
Grandfather in the lumber and paper trade
with a permit to travel to St. Petersburg!
Ordained rabbi but not into rabbinics
knew Hebrew spoke Russian
some German some Polish maybe some French
Grandmother, strictly Yiddish, kept the books
They had two sons and three daughters
I only know the sons' names
One was my father
The others?
Who knows . . .

They had a house
until the Twentieth Century knocked on their door
and ordered them out

Were they herded into the old ghetto area?
Were they starved to death?
Were they marched out in an *aktion*
forced to dig their own graves?

Were they killed in the huge pit of Ponar
their bodies later burned
by slave laborers
to leave no trace?
No trace. . . .

I can't light
a remembrance candle
since time, place, and circumstance
is anyone's guess . . .
all I can do is browse
among a choice of nightmares
all I can do is sketch
a picture in words
a kaddish out of time and place

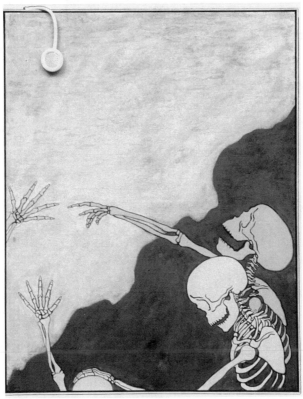

Figure 4.11   Marcia Annenberg   "Shower"

Figure 4.12   Lisa Kokin   "Transport"

LISTENING TO DEUTSCHLAND: 1980
Annie Dawid

Sharon sits on her hands in the cold compartment, sweating. She does not know why her train has stopped somewhere on the French-German border. A full moon lightens the black sky; there are no stars. Low mountains skirt the western horizon, and to the east, a long platform gleams silver. She can see dark trains under the eaves, laden with camouflaged jeeps and tanks, heading north into Germany. The trains move without noise; the only proof they exist is an occasional moonbeam refracting off the steel car beds.

To release her hands, Sharon lifts her hips, one at a time, and searches her vest for cigarettes, finding a crushed pack of Gauloise. The African man sitting by the door offers a match; he has been watching her tremble. They have not yet spoken to one another although they boarded the train together a few hours earlier in Paris, and are the only occupants of the compartment.

According to the French rail timetable, Sharon will have to wait one hour in Cologne before transferring to the Amsterdam express. Now, stopped at an isolated border in a foreign countryside, she watches the trains on the other side of the platform glide smoothly while hers remains stationary. She knows she will miss her connection and be forced to spend hours—maybe all night—in Germany.

She accepts the man's repeated offer of a light, draws on the cigarette and extends her pack to him. He looks not much older than Sharon, who is twenty, but he is relaxed, his features composed. A French paperback rests in his lap, but he does not read. Instead, he leans his head on the door and listens, his eyes closed.

Sharon's tongue sticks to the dry roof of her mouth like adhesive tape on tape; she needs something to drink. Someone is hawking Beck's Beer in the corridor, but Sharon cannot move. Her eyes and skin and nose announce her Jewishness to the reflection in the window, through which she sees the other train. The border guards slowly make their way through the many cars, asking question after question of some passengers, merely nodding at others, waving them through the procedure. She presses her lips to the cool glass, watching the endless procession of military cargo heading relentlessly into Germany. Without shutting her eyes she sees the cattle cars, the wisps of human bodies hanging from cracks in the slatted wagon walls. She sees numbers burned in flesh—the green-black ink on her cousin's arm. The trains go to Auschwitz, Bergen-Belson, Dachau, Treblinka.

She tastes salt in the corners of her mouth. The guard will read her passport and point an unforgiving finger at her. JEW, he will shout, and hustle her across the platform to the waiting death trains, to the journey north, into Germany, she has already taken in her dreams.

Ernst Weiss, her second cousin, keeps his yellow star pressed between the pages of a cracking photo album. "Juden" read the black letters imprisoned by the lines of the star of David. The sepia photographs show a genteel Berlin, a place of soft shadows where families pose in elegant parks. Sharon's grandparents, who died before the war, smile from the faded pages. Ernst and Egon, her father, stare obliquely into the distance, seeing something beyond the camera.

Her mouth leaves a ragged stain on the glass, and through the lines left by her parched lips, she can see the green-black military train, still moving, north into Germany.

Deutschland! The language makes her cringe, fills her throat with fear. The hard, clipped syllables of the approaching guards' voices form the same words she has heard in documentaries, in the speeches of Goebbels. *Mein Kampf.* Blut und Boden. Judenstrasse. Her father still refuses to speak the language; he left it in Europe when he escaped, and even with Ernst, he speaks only English. While Ernst and his wife survived Buchenwald, another cousin and his family did not. Now Ernst lives in Brussels and travels often to the United States. He is the only paternal relative Sharon has ever met. She had been on her way to visit him—her first trip abroad—when the Belgians went on national strike, and she was obliged to travel around that country to Amsterdam, via Cologne.

She imagines the guards wearing red and white armbands, the brilliance of their bright blue eyes and their yellow hair—the swastika branded on their character, an invisible but indelible tattoo. Hearing them now in the next compartment, their guttural voices biting through the wall behind her head, she examines her passport one more time. Although religion is not included in the data, it may as well read "Juden," because her name is Weiss, her hair brown, her eyes brown, her mother's maiden name Levy.

The door of the compartment slides open, banging against the jamb. A guard casts his gray eyes at her and says, JEW. He says, "Passport?" Sharon hands him the small blue book, careful not to touch his white,

white fingers. Another guard enters, and the two exchange words. THIS JEWESS, TAKE HER ACROSS TO THE OTHER TRAIN. They say, "A lot of Americans on this train." Sharon watches the dark convoy still passing silently in the night, moving without recourse toward its destination, its windows flying the red and white banners, the station draped in precise black swastikas.

JEW, the guard says. "You," he says, handing her the passport, turning his back to her, now confronting the African. They read his documents carefully, counting the many borders the man has crossed. They ask him a question, and the African responds, "Je ne parle pas Allemand." They try English, but he speaks no English. You speak French?" the first guard demands, and Sharon nods before she considers what she will have to do.

"Ask him where he is going," says the second guard.

She translates a battery of questions and responses, cursing herself for admitting she spoke French, guilty of being a collaborator. THEY WILL SHAVE HER HEAD. But the African remains calm. He lights a cigarette and offers one to Sharon, ignoring the uniformed men who obstruct his reach. She refuses, afraid her unsteady hands will give her away. Finally, the interrogation ends, and they leave, shouting at one another, slamming the door, which slides back open. The African shuts it gently, cutting the draft from the corridor.

"Ils sont horribles," she whispers and presses her forehead to the window, closing her eyes against the death trains still passing, against the red and white and black flags streaming in the German wind.

"Comme les autres," says the African as he covers his legs with his coat and makes a pillow of his arms, falling immediately asleep.

A week later, when the strike is finally settled, Sharon arrives in Brussels, ill and exhausted. In Cologne, she slept on a bench in the open-air platform, afraid to enter the station. Since then she has found it difficult to breathe, her lungs heavy and clogged. In Amsterdam she went to the various museums, and on her last day, guilt overcoming reluctance, to the attic where Anne Frank and her family lived in hiding before their deportation. She went there late in the afternoon; the sun was setting on the tree-lined canals, and a soft, yellow light filtered through the branches and shimmered on the water. Sharon's camera hung around her neck; she had taken many pictures of Dutch architecture, of the quaint narrow houses and tranquil waterways. But she could not photograph this house or this street, for she saw not the white-haired flower vendor or the handsome blond couple and their children, but the dark-haired, dark-eyed family being dragged into trucks, forced into trains, trains that would take them south, into Germany.

At the Brussels station Sharon telephones the number Ernst had written across the back of a photograph of his large family. Anna, his wife, tells her which tram to take, and soon Sharon is there, enveloped in the embrace of her distant cousins. "It is so good to finally meet the child of Egon," says Anna, her English thick and heavy. Sharon begs them to speak French with her; she needs to practice, she says. She cannot tolerate the German inflection, the blunt German edges of their words.

In their home she feels comfortable and cared for. Anna touches Sharon's warm forehead, discovers her chattering teeth and orders her to bed. Sharon protests but they tuck her in as if she were one of their own children, pushing the damp hair from her neck, smoothing the blankets around her.

Anna, too, wears the numbers on her forearm; they are graphite-colored, and the skin around them is tinted a jaundiced yellow, as if the ink had gotten into her blood.

Sharon sleeps all afternoon and on into the night—a fitful sleep, in which she dreams she awakens in Berlin in the house of her grandparents, hearing the voices of Egon and Ernst as young, eager boys in conversation at the dinner table, their words spoken in animated German.

When she opens her eyes it is late evening, and the apartment is filled with people; Ernst and Anna's four grown children, and their children. They have been there several hours waiting to meet her, eating and listening to music. Children run up and down the hallway, laughing and singing songs in French. She steps into the living room, dizzy but no longer feverish. "Hello, hello. Sharon, hello." They address her in English, and she answers in French, so that soon they are all speaking French. The eldest son, a dark man of forty, cradles his youngest child in his arms and looks happily around the room. "Das ist gut, nicht war? Sehr gut."

Sharon's face reddens, a peculiar mixture of pride and shame coloring her tone. "Je ne parle pas Allemand," she tells him.

Oh yes, he remembers now that her father refuses to speak German. "What a pity for you," he says.

In Belgium, the television news is available in Flemish and French, English and German. For Sharon's benefit, the channel is turned to the Parisian station. Although all the grandchildren speak French, Ernst and Anna and their children speak with one another in German, adding affectionate diminutives to ends of names: Marthe is Marthela, Gretel is

Gretelchen, and Peter is Peterlein. The endings soften the harsh sounds, make the words slightly more palatable, less similar to the words of the guards. Still, Sharon wants to believe with her father that the tongue itself is evil; she has never heard the German language spoken among loving people.

Occasionally one of the relatives addresses her in German, and again she must shake her head, repeat that she does not speak their language. They say it's too bad that Egon has denied her the gift of his native tongue, for there are some expressions that will not translate, some lovely expressions. "But surely your mother speaks Yiddish?" Anna asks. Again embarrassed, Sharon says no. Her mother is American-born, and knows few Yiddish words.

After the families have left, Anna and Ernst insist she go back to bed. "Sleep," they say. "Sleep mein Sharonchen, sleep well. Sweet dreams."

The days pass rapidly, and Sharon regrets she cannot stay longer, but she has made plans to meet a friend in Italy. She has grown accustomed to the interplay of languages in this Weiss home. "Naturlicht" is Anna's favorite word, and Sharon has come to like the sound of it, or perhaps it is Anna's enthusiastic manner that delights her. She admires their vast library, the books in French, German, English and Hebrew. Egon, a declared atheist, did not want his daughter to attend Hebrew school.

In the evenings, Ernst tells her stories about his youth, about the life he and Egon had known in Berlin before the war. It was a beautiful city, he says, with parks and statues and gardens full of birds. Surely she will visit Berlin, he says. "The cemetery where your grandparents are buried is still there. Their graves were part of the handful to survive the bombing. You should take flowers."

No, Sharon says; she has no intention of venturing into Germany. She tells them then about crossing the German border, about her terror and why she got sick, sleeping in the cold German air. Poor Sharon, they say, clucking their tongues, poor Sharonchen. We go there all the time to visit friends and to vacation in the mountains, they say. American Jews do not understand; it is not 1940 anymore.

When Sharon leaves she is well again. She promises to return some day; she wants very much to return. She hugs all of them goodbye, and last words are exchanged in French. The eldest son calls something in German as the train leaves the station, something which Sharon interprets as "Come back soon."

On the express to Milan she shares a full compartment with travelers from all over the world: two Australians, an Irish woman, a Spaniard and a Greek. The Australians have been everywhere already, and they tell stories about the best and worst places they've visited, which countries have been the most friendly, and which the least. Sharon contributes her story of how the Germans harassed the African but didn't ask her even one question.

"The German border ain't nothing compared to Italy's," says one of the Australians. "Those Italians tear up your luggage and ask you a hundred questions. You'll see."

Their train moves swiftly south, crossing the Italian border at midnight. They are stopped between stations for almost five hours while the border guards examine every page of every passenger's passport, grilling everyone. One of the guards suspects Sharon of being Italian because of her dark coloring; he interrogates her for a long time, repeating warnings about citizens evading taxes, warnings which Sharon does not understand. Finally he is satisfied she is telling the truth, and now Sharon must revise her conviction that Italian is the language of love.

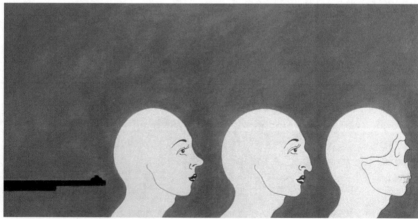

Figure 4.13   Marcia Annenberg   "Babi Yar/Bosnia"

FIFTIES DEFENSE PLANT, U.S.A.
"BUT NEVERTHELESS HITLER IS A REAL MAN!"
David Gershator

Aber Hitler ist doch ein mann!
I don't know German
don't want to learn it
but I know this phrase by heart—
my father works with
rehabilitated Nazis
imported factory and all
direct from Germany to far Rockaway
to do U.S. navy work.
Thanks to Germans
Father's family wiped out
Thanks to Germans
Father has a defense job
half the time defending himself:
"We've got to eat."

He comes home in a rage
and dances a spastic jig
imitating a co-worker baiting
the one and only
non-German on the floor
as slamming fist into palm
affirming with all his heart
Ja! Ve lost the var
Aber Hitler ist doch ein mann!
And the rehabilitated worker
goes back
to his bench and lathe
muttering about *der Jude*

imitating the imitator
I learn some German
whether I want to or not

JOINING THE STORY
Jason Sommer

The child's lateness was not yet resistance
to adult demands. He had merely forgotten
time and would be reminded by the hands
of his father who waited, so deep in his own story
of terror and loss that even the angry beating
of his heart was fear. When he saw the boy he joined

the ends of his belt in his hand and rushed to join
his child down the street before resistance
on either part. The child did not see the beating
coming, and if he saw it, he has since forgotten
his father's face then. The setting of his story
was lower: his father's legs, belt, whirling hands

between parked cars, his own warding hands
out of his picture of black curbs, sidewalk-joins,
one glimpse perhaps of a girl in the second story—
people all over the night and no resistance
in the warm air to the sounds of what's been forgotten
long since, some talk, a radio, a quick beating—

minor, and nothing like the beatings
the father got. One of them at the hands
of a young soldier may not be soon forgotten
because he will tell his son, and it will join
those things that are passed on about resistance.
The father struck the soldier in the story.

The man kept spitting in his food. That story
happened in a labor camp, and the beating
was severe, with no chance for more resistance
in a room where they had sticks in their hands,
the first soldier and the others who joined in.
Not killing him, though—perhaps they had not forgotten

some small thing yet, in all they had forgotten.
Later, he'll want the father to recall the story
of his little beating, though how can the son enjoin
him to? He cannot say, On this date my beating
happened—you frightened your son with your hands
and your belt. He knows his father's resistance

to memory. His father has forgotten that beating
when his son, late, took the story from his hands,
joining it after the worst and without resistance.

Figure 4.14   Barbara Leventhal-Stern   "Man in Striped Pants"

DREAM
Rochelle Natt

My Daughter's Dream occurring after meeting
her great uncle who, as a young boy, had been separated
from his family and sent to Auschwitz . . .

I was in a room
full of children
at the Museum
of Natural History
watching a man in white
dissect a cow's eye.
He held it high
for all to see.
The lights went out—
A loud speaker shrieked
"Follow the eye. Follow the eye.
It will take you to your mother,
your father, your sister, your brother."
The glowing eyeball
floated overhead.
I ran, bumping into children
darting here and there
sobbing, "Mama, Papa."
We reached a narrow door
lit with blue light.
Tiny yellow stars spelled out
Home.

Figure 4.15   Chandra Garsson   "Hold On"

GHOSTS
Elizabeth Rosner

even in winter
through snow deep as my thighs
my father walked me to synagogue
short-cutting through the parking lot of
the country club with (it was said)
a token Jewish member
and past the skating pond where
every other neighborhood child was free

in the coat room I removed
the pants I'd been allowed to wear
for the snow
my father already taking his place among
the davening men while I
slipped into a row of
silent women, off to the side where
we were not permitted to touch
the Torah or even its garments
with our unclean hands

my mother went shopping and
visited with her friends, not inclined
to participate in the ritual I had no
choice to refuse, although once
I stood my ground and said I
would not go with him and joined
my mother in the forbidden car
our hands touching money

I had learned how to recite the prayers
but never how to pray, not in my
own language and not
in my own voice
it was only later,

when I no longer walked with my father
that I found a moment of grace
when my hands hovered
above a pair of lit candles and I
whispered to the ghosts of every woman
who came before me, every blessed
touch of light

Figure 4.16   Cynthia Moskowitz Brody   "Many Ways to Tell the Story"

Figure 4.17   Chaim Goldberg   "We Dance"

BLOOD DANCES
Cynthia Moskowitz Brody

in memory of my grandmothers,
Pepi Hauer and Sarah Moskowitz

Somehow   in the midst of a womandance,
                whirling scarves and sacred secrets
a story steeped in sweetness
like strong, spiced tea   beckons.
The storyteller (dancer, teacher, sister)
struggles to contain this rogue spirit.
It is leaping now through fair,
transparent glassy skin,
most often shielded
from intruders.

She tells how she danced and sang
for her dead grandmother
How she praised her with words
like rose petals wrapped in gauzy melody
A silky path for her departing spirit
How lucky, both, for this final communion
this merging, an opportunity
to have gleaned wisdom
from one who has lived well and now
who has died well.

And we around her weep
strong salted tears for our own mothers
and grandmothers
and our daughters
and for our own unwelcome mortality.

And I am stricken with the sadness
that I never knew my own grandmothers
The one who died in the aftermath of malaria
and moments before her familiar world
would have crumbled
as a larger world began to swallow
those she loved.

What I have of her resides in stories
passed through her daughter to me
of this old world woman who shaved her
head at the marriage altar
as was her duty.
But the tale that lives in me, through me,
reflects that same devout and pious woman
setting candles on her kitchen floor
and weaving an exotic dance around them
as she had seen gypsies do that very night.

Her desire to capture
the fire of life
in movement
would weave its way
through the generations
where each woman that followed
could add her own flaming thread
and add to the tapestry
of passion.

Or that other tale, revealing untold yearnings
when she danced upon a wedding table
with the groom she could not make her own
as dictated by tradition
and heard him shout to all who could hear
"Now I don't care if I die!"
and she could carry that with her
to her death, his eternal gift,
which would be enough.

And my other grandmother
whose name I carry
along with a secret touchstone.
As her world closed in
she buried all her gold
and marked the spot for her son
who returned when she was only
smoke and memory

and found his treasured mother's
only remains.

He melted
all her dear familiar rings and chains
and made a bracelet, pink and solid,
timeless in its beauty
and now it is mine.
My reminder
of a grandmother I never knew
but who I wear upon my wrist
where I can feel my pulse
beating her name.

I too dance for my dead grandmothers
for their joy and their sorrows
lost loves, mothertears,
for their early leaving,
for the gifts they left me.
They call to me
bid me remember—
no graves to mark
I carry the stones in my heart.

Figure 5.1   Marcia Annenberg   "Resistance"

V.

Facing the Enemy

from SPEAKING TO ONE OF GERMANY'S SONS
Elizabeth Rosner

In the world where you and I
can face one another
like this,
nothing visible to tell us
apart,
familiar ghosts hover
at both our shoulders
whispering in the voices of
our parents
and the dead.

THE GERMAN LANGUAGE
Hans Jorg Stahlschmidt

I was born
a boy
with a name
with a nation
with a language
German
Deutsch
can you hear my accent ?
what is your first image ?
be honest

Nazi, Hogan's Heroes, Mercedes
fat pink people at the October Fest
intellectuals in gold framed glasses
Bach, Beethoven, culture, Nordic, cerebral ?

Ich spreche Deutsch

"No, no", your mother said
"we don't buy any German products
no Volkswagen, no Coo Coo clock"

I say *"Guten Tag"*
and you hear *"Achtung, Achtung, Achtung!"*

But this is the language I cried in
cried Mamma, Papa
this is the language I dreamt in
fell asleep to German lullabies
"Schlafe mein Kindchen schlaf ein"

This is the language I told
my first girl friend
"Ich liebe dich"

For me this is the language of love
is it for you
only the language
of hate ?

Figure 5.2 Harold Lewis   "Auschwitz"

Figure 5.3   Chandra Garsson   "Maya I"

THE LIMITS OF LANGUAGE
Hans Jorg Stahlschmidt

Leave one chair empty:
it belongs to the silent one
the one who cannot speak,
the one who cannot cry,
the one who does not scream anymore.

Be careful when you enter this place
where all words have been trampled,
let one word fall into the abyss
and just listen,
listen to the black echo
of language falling.

When you hear bones talking
and you see even death dying,
maybe then you understand
that it cannot be understood,
that there are no lips
to spell the alphabet of horror.

Try not to fill this void too soon:
walk silently through this valley,
there is only your breath,
all other languages have vanished
so please,
leave one chair empty.

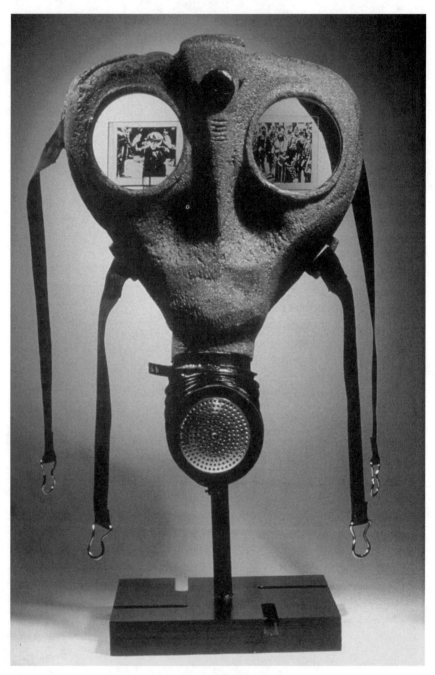

Figure 5.4   Harold Lewis   "Goebbel Prize Winner"

OBERSTURMBANNFUEHRER RUDOLF HOESS, FORMER COMMANDER OF AUSCHWITZ: AN ENCOUNTER
Harry Fiss

I sit in room 167
In the Captor's chair
Chewing nails and soul,
Waiting for boot-wearing Death
To make his entry,
Striding and bowing,
When I see a gray reflection
Nearing silently and stealthily.

As a moan beyond hearing
Escapes from my lips.
The interrogator eyes the page
On which I read the dreaded words.
An iciness that jells the air,
That turns my breath to frost,
An iciness no thermostat can thaw,
Causes me to turn my face
In the direction of the door
Which has led the gray Thing in.
I watch it stiffen with a chill
That paralyzes limbs and mind.

Moans and groans of millions of dead
Swarming in my brain like beehives.
How could you, Adonoi,
Let them die
And spare this one ?

He approaches.
Please don't let him near me,
Please don't!
Stop him, someone,
Please, please stop him

Before I freeze to death!
And here I am, the Conqueror,
and here he is, the Conquered.
And I sitting shivering in my chair,
While he calmly sits in his.

"I was foreman in a factory,"
I hear him say in a billowing voice.
"Mass production was our line of work.
We mass-produced masses of dead."
"Have a cigarette."

"Danke schoen."
A flicker of flame,
A puff of smoke,
Fumes that do not fumigate,
Like smoke coming from a chimney.
Below the chimney: a brick building,
And inside the brick building, ovens,
Ovens containing bones,
Human bones,
Ovens produced by Firma Topf,
Still doing business as usual.

"How many dead you said?"
"Two million dead."
"That's not what you said before."
Hoess shook his head
As curls of smoke rose from his mouth.
"Only two million were gassed."
"And the rest?"
"Well, you know, the usual thing,
Typhoid, dysentery, malnutrition.
We had an awful lot of typhoid cases in Auschwitz.
But only two million were gassed."
"I see. Change it then."
And then I heard that scratching sound,
That terrible scratching,
As without further ado,

Figure 5.5   Barbara Milman   "The Warsaw Ghetto"

Hoess crossed out three million and
Put two million
On top of the three million.
I heard a sigh coming across the table.
The facts were straight, at last.
It's the facts that count, the facts.

Clouds of blackness swept my mind.
Fire, ashes, cries of pain
Fill my daymare land.
And corpses piled so high
They form pyramids,
Not for the dead,
But pyramids of dead.

THE YOUNG GERMANS
Charles Fishman
for Sigrid Weinmann

Already at birth they seek forgiveness
a field of thorns flourishes
beneath their hearts

In the country of ghosts their first words
are silence they totter into darkness
as they walk

Their hometowns are absence and amnesia
which they wake from the way a black-out wakens
from the fuse box

And their childhoods—what breathes in them
but shame and anguish? The dark star of memory
rises in their blood

Who, then, has the power to save them?
Not the survivor of Belsen from Bensonhurst
who bakes for her young Aryan

Not the Ethiopian émigré in Ashkelon
who hums a tune more ancient than Rome
or Thebes

Who can release them but the Jews Grandfather
killed? Who can heal if not the Jews
only oblivion saved?

NOVEMBER RAIN
Hans Jorg Stahlschmidt
dedicated to Patricia

Today I am grateful for the rain—heavy like
milky sheets thrown down from heaven—the rain
that didn't come when the Wannsee-conference met
and the boxcars left for Bergen-Belsen.

These are the tears my parents never cried,
nor their neighbors, nor their uncles and co-workers,
nor the students when their classmates could not return
to school, when their neighbors were picked up in
midnight fog, when books disappeared from libraries
and stores closed for ever while storm-troopers
marched proudly up and down clean streets.

These are the tears I cried with you, German and Jewish
tears washing down together the dust from the Hebrew
letters on the gravestones in Prague, stones stacked on
top of each other as if even in death there was no room
to be, these tears falling onto the deaf tunnel walls in
Theresienstadt and on the Appellplatz in Dachau.

These are the tears that mourn absence, the life
that could have been, the richness of friendships never
made, the Jewish quarters which vanished, the German-
Jewish thoughts never thought, the sound of Yiddish
which could have warmed the long Prussian winters.

This is a grief which does not have a grave
nor a monument nor a museum; a grief without
a name, a photograph or a song. It is the grief of
murdered possibilities, of a strangled unborn,
of books not written, of a painting burnt to ashes,
of orchards which never bloomed, it is the loss
of a brother and a sister I never had.

VISIT TO THE FATHERLAND
Hans Stahlschmidt
for Patricia

We all had a lot to drink—wine and beer with
a heavy German meal. My father—neglected—
became cranky like a child while the darkness was
falling warm and soft upon the poplars and our
family gathered around the large dinner table.
My father suddenly rising above the permanent thick haze
of his mind turned to you and I translated that he was glad—
you were with me—you an American woman whose country
was once an enemy and I said und eine Jüdin,
yes he said after a long pause, eine Jüdin

You were looking at him with your large green eyes
as if thousands of your tribe were looking through you
as I translated: I am sorry for what the Nazis and the
Germans did to your people, it was so wrong, so inhuman
And I want you to know that I never did anything to
any Jew. He took your hand from the green and white checkered table
cloth and you both cried and my sisters cried.
An old warrior had finally reached out before his mind
faded into a lasting night. I sat still, looking across
the darkening lake and the gray silhouette of the Alps
trying to catch the last vanishing light and I was unsure
if I could fully believe what he had said, knowing that
there was no one left to erase my doubts. When we
walked out I held you tightly as if to press your body
into mine leaving marks no one could ever erase.

PLEASANT DEMEANOR
(*KLAUS BARBIE, THE BUTCHER OF LYON, IS DEAD.*)
Adam D. Fisher

There he was with his sweet little smile,
there he was with his pleasant demeanor.
Look at his pictures,
the face of a man you'd want to know,
like the neighbor who waves,
the man who sell suits.
But he was the one,
yes him.
He was the one who killed
thousands of Jews
thousands of children,
thousands of Jewish children.
He, really, he was the one
the man with that smile.
He was the one.
And if he, yes he,
with his face
with that expression
with that smile
with that pleasant demeanor
could kill
and kill again
and again
would kill thousands of times
maybe your neighbor
or even you
or even I
could kill too.

Figure 5.6   Harley Gaber   "Die Plage" (Section 2)

GERMANS AND JEWS
Hans Jorg Stahlschmidt

As the sun has to sink and the moon
and all hope far below the horizon
our hearts have to be full of night first
and we have to feel the fear
before we can feel a timid love.

How can I not be heavy
when I am with you
like ancient miners we have to descend
into this dark quarry where bones sleep
restlessly and prayers and screams
are entombed in the earth.

We have to labor hard to make
the gray coal shine and to find our
faces in this broken stone
we have to be heavy first before we
can find the lightness of the morning rain
and be children again playing in a Bavarian
meadow or on the beach near Tel Aviv.

We have to trust the heaviness as
we trust the sun setting
as we trust falling asleep
as we trust the fever to cure
our sweating dreaming bodies.

MUNICH. MAY, 1987
Bonnie Salomon

I took a train to Dachau today. A commuter train, actually, that left from the center of town. I took a train to Dachau today, after I'd eaten a bratwurst for lunch. I found the tourist information booth beneath the Glockenspiel and asked, "How do I get to Dachau?" She explained the route. I said, "Danke" and was off.

I went to Dachau today. With map in hand, Nikon at my side, passport in pocket, I was quite the tourist americaine. Dachau is simply another stop on the Munich subway map. Perhaps it is not that extraordinary to ask directions for Dachau. But for me, it seems like finding a stop called, "Hell," or "Inferno." The name seems out of place to me, to resonate with meaning. Perhaps that is all it will mean in the future—Dachau the subway stop.

When the train pulled into the stop, I looked at the signs. Naturally, they read, "Dachau," in the typography of the Munich subway system. I was amazed. Again, it seemed as unnatural as having a subway sign marked "Death."

I discovered that Dachau is more than the memorial. There really is a town, Dachau, and to my chagrin, I found it to be a pleasant little place. The streets and houses are well-kept. Children cross the streets and laugh. I think to my self, "How can they live in Dachau? How can people bear to live here?" But it is 1987, and Dachau is a small town with a well visited memorial. The name "Dachau" is everywhere: buses, restaurants, signs. Again this seemed unnatural. A town named for death? No, this town is very much alive"

I found my way to the "Gedankenstatte," following signs. I go past manicured lawns and single family homes, until I follow the last sign. I turn left, and enter Dachau concentration camp.

There they are—the watchtowers. There it is—barbed wire. There they are—the lagers. I tell myself "You're really here. You're in a camp." I look at the trees. They're pretty in the breeze. Were they pretty forty years ago, too?

First, I go to the lager. There they are—the wooden racks that passed for "beds." They seem familiar. I have seen the pictures, it seems, forever. But these are reproductions. In fact, the entire lager is a reproduction. A sign says that after the war, the barracks were found to be "derelict" (whatever that means), and so were torn down. I think the

Figure 5.7 Rosa Naparstek   "Song Of Atonement"

Germans were too ashamed to let the truth stand,. These barracks are too clean, the paint is fresh. It feels fake, it feels like the truth has been touched up.

I walk down the "road" between the barracks. How many people walked here before me? There is a patch of grass in front of the foundations of the barracks. A man is mowing the grass in front of barrack #8. How absurd. Now they mow the grass. Now they care. If they had cared for the thousands who died here—

At one end of the camp stand three memorials. I go to the Jewish "chapel." It is a narrow stone structure, quite tall, with an opening at the top. Light falls into the chapel, but it is an eerie light, like the light hitting a dungeon wall.

In front of the chapel, I grab a stone and put it in my pocket. I know this stone was placed here when the camp was "landscaped" for visitors. Still, it is a stone from Dachau. A souvenir for an American tourist. The dead are all around me. I am in one big cemetery. I grab a stone. I grab at memories.

There is a sign in a corner of the camp. "Krematorium," it reads. It is open 9 to 5. This way to death, it should say. This way to the end of your days, to the end of the Jewish race, to the end of the world.

I cross a narrow stream and go past some lovely trees and grass. There must be many bodies underneath this lovely grass, I think.

I see a brick building, not very large at all, almost like a house. The door is open, and there is enough light to find that I am staring into an oven. Oh, God, an oven. (The structure of nightmare, a sinister image of the twentieth century.) There are about four brick ovens. I am face to face with a crematorium. This is it, this is not a story, not a picture. Tears form in my eyes, but I am too self-conscious to let them flow.

The room with the ovens leads to a "disinfection room." The walls are clean. A sign reads "Do not write on the walls." I touch the wall. How many grabbed onto these walls? Now they are spotless.

There are times in life when words do not suffice, and I had one today. I will try anyway, lest I forget. At least these words will summon up the emotions I had at this time. This time I refer to is my entrance to the next room. I walked into the gas chamber.

The gas chamber seemed to be a smaller room than the others. The ceiling seemed lower, and light was dim. There were vents on the walls. Oh, God, I thought. I am in the gas chamber. I am here, in this place where the world changed forever. Here, my people died. Here, I would die. I was meant to die here. I was meant to be burned in the next room.

Again, the room is clean. I press my palm against the wall. The wall is cool. I try to touch this cursed past. I press the wall of the gas chamber, like the thousands before me. But I will leave. I will walk out. This is 1987 and Dachau is a subway stop.

(God, let me out of this place, out of this country. I vow to be a Zionist forever.)

I cross the stream and am back near the barracks. There is a building on my right with a door of metal bars. The top of the door reads "Arbeit Macht Frei" The three words that equal hell. I pass through the door, and give it the finger. A child, I am. Ha, I think, to hell with you, I'm still here. You didn't wipe out the Jews. I'm alive, and am living the good life in America. We'll multiply and thrive. To hell with you. I'm a Jew who will walk out of the gas chamber and give the finger to your goddamned door with its poisonous slogans. Then I think if I gave that door the finger in 1941, would they have shot me? Would that gesture have meant my death?

The museum is next. It is extensive and filled with Germans and tourists. Good. The young need to know. It will mean less to them. But they should know. I go through the museum slowly, but my travelling companion hurries me. He wants to get to a music store by 5, I know. He doesn't say that, but I know. At first I am angry. This is my history, my heritage, so let me take my time. You could never understand how I feel now. (How self-righteous.) Then I think maybe it is time to leave. It is time to leave death, and reenter the world of the living. This is 1987, and the record stores close by 5 p.m. I am not a survivor, I was not here. I am an American Jew, and my life did not end here. My life story is still to be lived.

I left Dachau. I took two photos—the watchtower, and the door. I wanted to remember. I wanted to see it all in color, not in the archives of black and white. I walked out of Dachau today, and went to the subway stop. I took one last photo—the subway stop sign "Dachau." I wanted to remember that this is 1987, and that Dachau is a subway stop, and children call it home.

DU! ICH? JA, DU, DU, MEINE LIEBE ÜBERMENSCH . . .
Gabriel Ariel Levicky

You don't have bodies
      hanging over your TV news & playing with on and off . . .
You don't have bodies
      lying under your kitchen table & peeling your last orange . . .
You don't have bodies
stuck in the refrigerator & there is still room for Schaefer and Schlitz . . .

You don't have bodies
put together like a necklace of Korczak's kids from the Children's Republic . . .

You don't have bodies
on the front page of Playboy staring at you with one frozen eye & mouth
foolishly open . . .

You don't have bodies
      waiting with at the bus station & looking for small change . . .
You don't have bodies
      sitting in your car at the gas station for unleaded gas only . . .
You don't have bodies
      in your bar sipping spicy bloody Mary . . .
You don't have bodies
      going with you to the church where you can see angels with
      round innocent faces . . .
You don't have bodies
      while you are with a woman & she closes her eyes . . .
You don't have bodies
      with you just a few seconds before your climax & now you
are ready to sleep . . .
You don't have bodies
      when you don't have time for dreams . . .
      but they are there . . .
      Where you left them . . .
      Waiting for you . . .
      Me?
      Yes, You, You . . .
      Meine liebe Übermensch!

TO THE GERMAN TOURIST'S DAUGHTER
Shula Robin

It was June or July
1975
at Toronto General Hospital
when a cry for help
pierced the air
seeking a communicator
between the gravely ill
German tourist,
his daughter and doctor.

The young German woman said:
"I flew in from West Berlin
to take my father home
dead or alive.
Thank you again and again.
Your German is so fluent,
is your homeland Germany too?"
"No, no,
I came to Canada from Poland.
Normally my mouth never, never opens
in German
to people of my generation
because of the inevitable question:
Is He the one, are They the ones
who turned my parents
to ashes, to soap,
and my brothers and my folk?"

"I know, I know," she cried out.
"With this guilt I will have to die!
Home in West Berlin,
watching with my husband
programs on television,
we whisper to one another:
Do you think my gentle parents

did it too?
Is it possible my beloved parents
murdered viciously,
counting, one, two, one, two . . . ?"

The German woman's words
gave me a tremor
a quiver
touched deeply my soul.
Oh God,
we are both tormented souls!
I don't know your name
neither do you know mine
but we will never forget
one another
and the conversation
at Toronto General Hospital
was it in June or July
1975

MUNICH 1980
Liselotte Erlanger Glozer

Not as a traveler
      visitor
        nor observer
but as archaeologist
      of past emotions
I enter the café

Above me   windows
from where   years ago
a child I scanned
the trolley stop
for return
      of father
      arrival
of favorite aunt cousins
      friends

Gone. Few claimed by age
others bones   teeth   smoke
They left me
to purge from memory
      the dead
as if they never
      had lived

Shall I paint the past
      in pinks blue
      butter yellow?
Be more forgiving
      than their Christ?

At the trolley stop
an old woman descends
crosses the square
The waiter serves me coffee
and cake

I shall drink
I shall eat
I shall pretend
I eat the bread
of forgiveness.

Figure 5.8 Elly Simmons "Survivor"

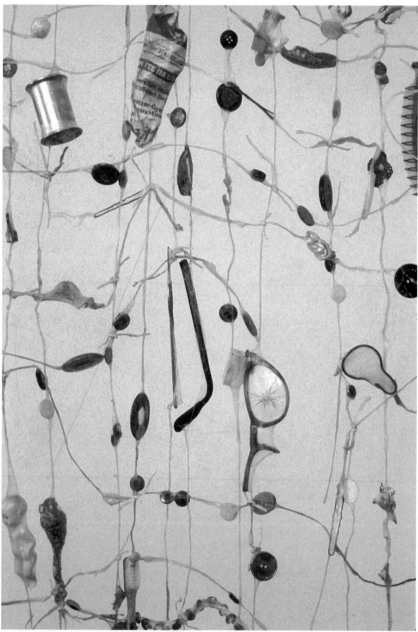

Figure 5.9   Lisa Kokin   "My Trip to Buchenwald #1" (detail)

WHAT WE WANT FROM OUR ENEMIES
Myra Sklarew

Not retribution but what they've used: a metal
map box, food rations, a scrap

of cloth, wood from a fire, the living
ember, even a trip wire

fine as a hair, thread to explosives—anything
still bearing a trace of the enemy's body.

The Vietnam vet in the dark theatre warns: *Don't
touch it!*—when the soldiers reach

for the container belonging to the Viet Cong.
Too late: they are blown

to bits. *We wanted to know who they were.*
When the daughter of a Holocaust survivor lived

For some days with the son of a Nazi, she asked
putting her arm through his: *How*

can I hate this man? He is like me . . .

So we crawl back
along the ledge of death

to this incongruous place: we touch the Nazi sons
as though they could lead us to the lost lives

of our parents, as though by knowing
them, we could at last witness the pure agony

of our mothers and fathers that we might pull them in
from the waters of their drowning.

SPEAKING TO ONE OF GERMANY'S SONS
Elizabeth Rosner

This is not about apology:
what, after all,
can possibly be forgiven
between us
when none of it
and all of it
belongs here.

In the world where you and I
can face one another
like this,
nothing visible to tell us
apart,
familiar ghosts hover
at both our shoulders
whispering in the voices of
our parents
and the dead.

If you were a window and I
at the glass
tried to see through you,
wouldn't I be faced
with my own face,
myself in the glass
looking back and through and beyond?

I'd see your ghosts there too,
in uniforms maybe with dogs
and maybe terrified,
maybe trying to shape
the word Why or even
No.

And if not, if your ghosts
have blood on their hands,
what can I say about that?

Did any of us ask
to be born into this place
or that one?
Could our fathers know
that we would come after them
trying to make our own mistakes
come out right?
Don't our mothers hope
that our sleep is sweet
and untroubled,
that our hands don't tremble
when we stretch them toward
one another?

CULTURAL EVENTS
(ARBEIT MACHT FREI)
Ruth Daigon

Our season tickets stamped on our arms,
we sit among the perfumed furs and patent leather
in our striped uniforms, waiting.

Footlights glow. She appears.
Opening chords lift off
like birds flying backwards.

Long skeins of sound
wrap loosely around listeners.
Phrases gleam brighter than
searchlights on prison towers.

High notes strict as flames
in burning synagogues
singe us in our seats.

Her burnished voice,
her tempos locked in marrow,
the even rhythm of her breath
moves us toward the showers.

She sings of spring melting shards of winter,
of summer burning along branches,
of seeds spiraling to earth
as light as babies falling in slow motion
into soft beds of soil.

The texture of her voice
rubbed smooth by each new season,
ours grown thin as parchment.

Now, she carves sound out of
a country of bare surfaces

where we pound rocks into pebbles
paving roads to Treblinka,
Buchenwald.

And when she sings of love
hidden circuits warm our bodies
packed in vats of ice.

The audience rises with applause,
the stage buried in bouquets.
She bows.

But from somewhere in the wings,
a voice hums lullabies of barbed wire
and the string quartet rests between numbers
waxing their bows.

Figure 5.10   Elly Simmons   "Dybbuk"

IF YOU COULD LICK MY HEART
Hans Jorg Stahlschmidt
dedicated to Itzhak Zuckerman
a leader of the Warsaw Ghetto uprising

There was no bridge from Auschwitz back
to the world. We made it up. We tried to find
tales of good and heroic triumph; we attached hooks
and ropes to the bottomless abyss of evil. But the ones
who survived helplessly watching their brother or
child murdered were never again at home in the world:
Primo Levi, Tadeusz Borowski, Jean Amery, Paul Celan—
the list is longer than Schindler's.

So let us be careful to know that we are the ones
who were not there, that we are the ones who put
words were there was nothing, put a light
were there was only an unending star-less night,
put hope in that place where human hair piled
up to a mountain of despair, where God's hand
remained motionless behind smoke-filled clouds.

Our imagining can barely touch the outer reaches
of those experiences, but it allows us to dilute
the deadly waters of that truth. "You ask me for
my impressions," Itzhak Zuckerman replied,
"if you could lick my heart, it would poison you."

VI.

Chosen

from THE BREAKING OF THE GLASS
Jason Sommer

God gave Moses a mouth
that brimmed with glass
that when he spoke
his pain was keen
and the blood came to his face.
This was His way of saying:
I am the Lord
My voice is in
the gusting of the wind
and the stuttering of men
and the breaking of the glass

Figure 6.1   Dorrit Title   "Captives"

HOW TO READ HOLOCAUST POEMS
Charles Fishman

The sun beats down
its cryptic ode
to violence
and desire rides high
in the saddle
of the cold wind:
tufts and drifts
of straw,
slivers of soap
and charred bone.

Forgiveness is not
the theme
nor is despair.
Only the first hush
matters—
the rest, a voice that
drones
at a deaf ear.

Though each verse
rings true,
the poem is a lie:
only one's ache
to speak
matters—
only one's hunger
to waken

BLESSED ART THOU, NO-ONE
Myra Sklarew

> "No one kneads us again of earth and clay,
> No one incants our dust.
> No one.
> *Blessed art thou, No-One.*"   -Paul Celan

If I reach after you
into the darkness

will you stay put against my hand
or will I scrape against

the steady pulsing
of my own fingers

This day   held up
like a flag of warning

no-one made of words
soaked into the earth

stray words from the shrunken mouths
of those who sat down

in the forest
unlacing their shoes

Used up words
that we leaning

across a table wanted
to say to you

before the table
turned into a gun

before the chair fled
its house

If we attach the words
to our feet like a boot

will you walk on them
will they cry out

under you
like a woman

Will the faces of gravestones
call to you

when they are hammered into stairs
or set into roads

when the tanks run over
their names

Are you made of words no-one
shall I give you a name

or must your provisions
be metal and rope

or something to carry
these papers

so that you may cross
a border into your own life

Figure 6.2   Dorrit Title   "Memorial"

LOST FACES
Leatrice Lifshitz

FROM THE ROMAN VISHNIAC PHOTO EXHIBIT:
A VANISHED WORLD

buying lost faces
as if they were some treasure
a trophy to save, to save

are they saved

buying lost faces
forty dollars for the book
with glossy black and white blood
and galactic tears

are they saved by being sold

buying lost faces
that line of long steps
bones
given to each star

does saving them save us

buying lost faces
Jews have many faces
a quarrel
and its prayer

faces to buy

buying lost faces
hidden in someone else's
mouth, stone, tree
eyes

facing the faces

buying lost faces
from the mud-maker
a song we sing
a game we play

<u>the face we love</u>

buying lost faces
to be buried
in kinder
graves

the bodies . . . god
has bought them
all

Figure 6.3   Marcia Annenberg   "Wedding Party 1941"

ALMOST A LOVE POEM
Yehuda Amichai

Translated by Chana Bloch

If my parents and yours
hadn't emigrated to the Land of Israel
in 1936,
we would have met in 1944
there. On the ramp at Auschwitz.
I at twenty,
you at five.

Where's your *mameh*,
your *tateh*?

What's your name?
Haneleh.

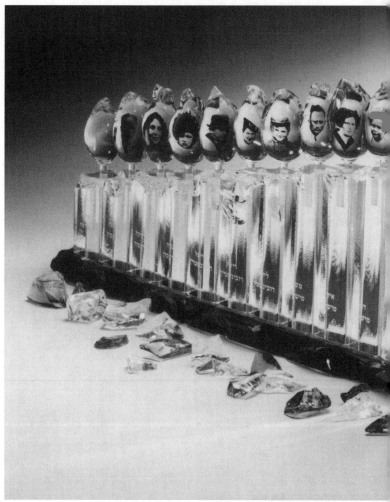

Figure 6.4 Toan Klein   "Listen to the Flames"

THE BREAKING OF THE GLASS
Jason Sommer

He observed that the rabbis present were very gay.
So he seized a costly goblet . . . and broke it before them.
Thus he made them somber.

Talmud

Make me a wedding glass of crystal
to outlast the shrillest pitches
of a solid scream,
the heel above the temple
and the people dragged
along the shards.

One true form of tears
is heaps of glass—
from windows with their faces kicked-in
and the family's crystal
and all the unlucky mirrors of the houses
now with their several million faces
that cannot reflect.

God gave Moses a mouth
that brimmed with glass
that when he spoke
his pain was keen
and the blood came to his face.
This was His way of saying:
I am the Lord
My voice is in
the gusting of the wind
and the stuttering of men
and the breaking of the glass.

ABUSE
Dahlia Ravikovitch

Translated by Chana Bloch and Ariel Bloch

In that place,
one of those places,
the flowers were gnawed to shreds,
devoured like prey,
dogs bared their teeth,
barked in their fury—
the flowers were gnawed to shreds.
My God,
was there beauty!

In that place,
different from all those places,
they were like sunflowers
trailing in the sun—
when they lifted their heads
their fragrance followed the sun.
And hours after they were torn apart.
Even after they died,
that soul still burned in them.
My God,
was there abuse!

Figure 6.5   Deborah Trilling   "No Killing"

G-D POEM
Juliet Zarembski

The laws teach us to cover our eyes
when we say that you, G-d, are one
and we learn the words by heart
concentrating on the red lit lines
beneath our cupped dark hands

and tradition teaches us to get drunk on
holidays until we cannot tell the
difference between the hero and the villain.

G-d poems to you rain by the thousands
from crops to grow in drought
and for thirsty children at the hands
intravenous tubes who die
from dehydration

but this poem is not a prayer
it is not another letter to add
to the book of scholars
I am not a scholar
I am a woman, forbidden to touch
the tree stem of the Torah
the tree of knowledge,

My hands are stained red from
Eve's apple
and I am forever unclean

but this poem
(as I choose to call it)
is my sacrifice
the words burn the pages with
my fear
and in the temple of my thoughts

I lay open on the altar of Abraham
to sanctify myself unto you

I have fallen forever in debt
to you
(it happened when the rain finally came
and my sister could take out
the tube from her nose)
and I have been pierced in the ear*

The words blacken my lips
forever dry from disuse

only wet with kisses I save for
you, the books dusted two half moons
where my lips touched it.

But poems to G-d rain by the thousands
and women ripe for marriage
should spend less time praying
conserving their energy for their husbands,
but I am forever given to you
bound by the same shreds that bound Isaac

and he was saved.
He became the founder of a great nation.
I do not ask for anything,
well, maybe,
just for rain
a little rain
to wash the blackness, the dust
from these withered lips.

*It was customary in ancient Israel for slaves to have their ear pierced as a sign of
possession.*

ASUR
Juliet Zarembski

Black hats twirl like tops
as their owners, stern men in wool overcoats
totter by

one by one
or ten by ten
they scurry past
their black garbs blend together
like my pen's new ink
black and smooth,
spread across the street like
the smudge across my page.

A smudge across the street
dyed with the finest of rabbinical thought
twisted earlocks coil like
serpents right out of Genesis
and from quivered lips one could make out
the sounds of antiquity.

Red beards, brown coarse straw hair
weigh down ghost faces
reminders of a history sad to the taste
a bloody aftertaste of Auschwitz
of burnt Shtetle Europe
the burden of a people on such bony shoulders!

And the women with shaved heads,
not shaved by the Nazis,
shaved by a brother or sister as a wedding gift
to remind her she has but one husband
who need not notice a curl, a wisp, a strand
need not look, just have as a whole
like a fish on Sabbath night
and love, because it is decreed—

with their daughters in braids
like challah loaves
mending and sewing the blackness

feeling the black wool,
hearing the dead in the voices of their papas
murmuring and swaying
and holding responsibility in their hands
like silver candle sticks

Time does not enter the
narrow cobblestone alleyways of the righteous;
the penalty for improper dress
is a sharp round stone in the back,
and time knows not of woolen coats and black hats
just the cloth of a secularist
without a home or a past.

Figure 6.6   Lauren Herzog Schwartz   "Klezmer Dreams"

JEWISH MUSIC IN THE CAMPS
Lyn Lifshin

had to be
held in the mind

the nightingale
of the ghetto,
Maryasha Eisenstat
was shot by S.S. in 1942

Israel Faieshes
organized children's
choirs at
Lodz, Warsaw
and Vilna. Israel Glatch
wrote theatrical
songs and performed
them before his
end at Treblinka

Abraham Step started
the Jewish Music
Institute in Vilna
taught ghetto songs

died in Estonia
Mordecai Gebirtig
sought out and murdered
for spreading music

Sephardic Jews sang Ladino
sang as they lost
their lives

so much music
lost   what is left
like a bit of

I SIT AT MY PIANO
Cecile Low
in memory of Sonja Haber

I sit at my piano and play,
mi mi sol mi mi do . . .
Sonja's own moving song
which she composed
when she was thirteen,
in Antwerp, our home town.
I, a gray-haired woman,
play it
and Sonja appears.

She takes me by the hand
and out we go for a walk
and into the park.
We row on its lake,
our hair fluttering in the wind
and singing her song.
In a sidewalk café
we order some lemonade.
We sip it,
chatting about our teachers,
the one she loves the one I love.

We dance together
our first waltzes.
Together we swim and dive
and bike and hike,
the wind caressing us,
the sun smiling at us,
the flowers emitting
their most fragrant aroma.
When we pass,
they all know us,
the inseparables,
always together.

Except
when only one of us
goes up the chimney at Auschwitz.

Mi mi sol mi mi do,
re re sol sol mi do . . .
I sit at my piano and play.

GIFT OF THE RASPBERRY
Lyn Lifshin

Don't poison your day
she smiles,
her black eyes bright.
Use the beacon of the past,
the darkness
to outline the present
that we often take
for granted.
I saw in the work camp
beauty: my friend,
though starving,
fifty pounds,
found a raspberry—
kept it in her pocket all day
for me.
What kept me going?
It was the memory
of the ordinary day,
the kind I'd, then,
have thought boring.
It was all I dreamt of
behind barbed wire.
Days after the gift
of the raspberry
Sasha gave me
the biggest gift:
on the Death march
she begged,
unable to go on,
though I could have
curled up next to her,
that I must go on

WHERE ARE MY CHICKENS
Lyn Lifshin

She's searched
all over town, past
the beach party on
the river, but
she still can't
find them. "I must,"
Yaffa Eliach says,
"find my chickens."
She's scanning
photographs, 1500
pictures in Ejszszki,
Lithuania, she's
standing in the
tower of faces at
the Holocaust Museum,
the crunch of snow
in Lithuania still
in her ears, the
smell of the
apple trees lingers.
Now a grandmother,
she leans forward,
pivots, looks for
the shot of a grinning
girl surrounded by
chickens. "There,"
she says spotting the
4 year old in a
gingham dress. It's her
as a child, in 1941,
snapped the morning the
Nazis marched into
her village. Three

months later only 39
of the 3500 escaped the
bullets of the Einsatzgrubper,
the mobile killing squad.
In two days they were
stripped, shot
and shoved into bloody
ditches. Yaffa Eliach
has dug up their memory,
obsessed by her goal to
collect a picture of
every Jew from the shtetl
she traveled, bartered
bought, smuggled faces.
"there's my uncle, most
eligible bachelor in town,"
she points brightly at a
handsome man in a bathing
suit "There's Freddy's
farewell party when he
 left for America. There's
the swim team, the town
rabbi. I must find him."
For years she says later,
her family lived in a
nearby cave under a pig
sty, their only light,
stories about weddings,
graduations and holidays.
When she went back to
Lithuania in 1988 she
realized the Jews had
died a double death.
First physically, then
their memories. The
cemeteries were demolished,
tombstones ground up and
used to pave roads. But
in the photographs their

Figure 6.7   Denise Satter   "Angel of the Light"

faces come back. Yaffa's
family rescued 100 photos,
some she smuggled out
of Europe in her shoes
as a girl, some her
father found, hid, some
his brother hid strapped to
his body when he jumped
ship and swam ashore to
Palestine. "we have, she
says, prisoners in striped
suits, cattle cars. It's
easy to show evil. But how
do you convey the beauty of

the human soul? I didn't
see them as bones and
skulls, I wanted to show
them going to school,
skating, picking flowers."

Figure 6.8   Chaim Goldberg   "The Last Way"

SPEAKER FOR THE DEAD
Roald Hoffmann
> in memory of Primo Levi

Shall this heap of gold teeth
pulled root and all by kapos
speak for them? They once bit
a sugar cube for every cup of tea
and raspberries. They remember
too many Sabbath sweets.

If not this, shall the unmuted
witness of man's base twist speak
of Mengeles and Ivans, freezing
experiments, the butt of a gun?
In the same camp a man
gave me two crusts of bread,
and some rare earth metal chips
sold well as flints.

Who shall speak for the dead?
I, said the dazzling southern day.
I waft you the smell of a favela.
I bring you news from a doctor.
And I, said my night. I give you
eels of comparison
with those who didn't come back.
I speak for the dead
when I take away your breath
when I wake you every day at 5
the time you woke in the camp

Figure 6.9   Chaim Goldberg   "Ode to Joy"

TO MY CHILDREN
Susan Terris

Instead of using the staircase,
Risk the tendrilled stalks of ivy
And drop into the muddy copse below.

Your great grandfathers understood mud
As they slogged from village to village
Peddling pots and ribbons and scissors.

They knew days with no light, nights
With no heat, years with no safety—
Years of pogroms, famine, and loss.

But still, you may collar their essence
If, shaking pearls from your ears,
You can know wet boots and windfall.

Figure 6.10 Elly Simmons   "My Mother, My Daughter—a Tree of Life"

Descriptions of Art

Figure 1.1   *The Roots of the Pain Go Deep*   Barbara Leventhal-Stern. 3' x 3' Oil on canvas, 1992.
An illustration of the artist's feeling that the trauma of the Holocaust has permeated the psyche of all Jewish people and penetrated their souls.

Figure. 1.2   *Invisible*   Sharon Siskin. 25 x 40 x 5" Mirror, wood, paper, glasses, magnifying glass, 1995.
This piece is about how anti-Semitic words and phrases are often used in the presence of Jews, either out of ignorance or because we don't always look like the image that the rest of the population might have of us. The three reflective mirrored panels read: but you/don't look/ like a/JEW. Hanging from the lower frames are copies of the stars that the Nazis used to identify Jews at different concentration camps in Europe during the Holocaust.

Figure 1.3   *You Can't Drown It Out*   Barbara Leventhal-Stern. 18 x 23" Etching, 1985.
An etching with collage elements. Within the figure of the rabbit is a photograph of a small girl with a suitcase, waiting to be deported. The "It" in the title refers to the memory of the Holocaust.

Figure 1.4   *Our Bones Don't Belong to Us*   Leah Korican. 18 x 24", 1994. Collection of Alexandra Feit. This piece is about the continuity of life. We don't control our own legacy nor do we create ourselves from whole cloth. Photograph: Kate Cameron.

Figure 2.1   *Skinhead Arbeit Macht Frei XVIII*   Harold Lewis. 46 ½ x 20 x 25" Mixed media, 1995.

The image depicted in the "eye" of the skinhead was of a woman being restrained at the sight of her daughter being raped during the recent Bosnian atrocities. This, coming at the time of widespread rising of skinhead violence and appearance of revisionist writing about the Holocaust, was the inspiration for creating the piece. Glued over the surface of the head are reproductions of international skinhead propaganda in their original languages. The pendant hanging from the chain is a hand carved grenade.

Figure 2.2   *Unearthing* (detail)   Lisa Kokin. Mixed media installation (shovels with text burned into the handles or etched into the blades), cement, pigment, 1990.

Unearthing consists of twenty-three shovels embedded in clay and cement, each one containing an anti-Semitic phrase or word either etched into the blade or burnt into the handle. This lexicon of hatred runs the gamut from the overt "kike" to the subtle and more contemporary "pushy," and also includes phrases like "Jewish American Princess" and definitions from an old dictionary in which Jew is used as a verb and an adjective.

Figure 2.3   *Unearthing*   Lisa Kokin (see above)

Figure 2.4   *If Love Had Wings* (detail)   Rosa Naparstek. 34 x 22 x 16 ½" Mixed media with text & sound, 1994.

This piece connects two children of war across five decades, both holding dolls, with one trying to reach out to the other in hopes of providing comfort and love. Photograph: Joe Schopplein

Figure 2.5   *Persephone*   Chandra Garsson. 33 x 29 x 15" Mixed media, 1993.

Persephone was kidnapped by Pluto to be queen of the underworld, Hades, allowed to visit the surface of the world once a year in the personification of Spring. She is portrayed as a child cradling a skull. (her own death?) The life cycle from egg to mature human is depicted on the pelvis/pedestal on which she stands. The Holocaust, viewed through this sculpture, is a view of the life process from conception to death to which we are bound and helpless in the face of the cruelty imposed, not by nature or God, but by humanity.

Figure 2.6   *The Order Of Things*   Rosa Naparstek. 39 x 21 x 13"
Mixed media with text, 1994.
Juxtaposes the totalitarian experience, either a child's or an adult's,
with another world of innocence and unity. Photo: Joe Schopplein

Figure 2.7   *Auschwitz #6*   Barbara Milman. Fig. 3.8 12 x 6" Linocut,
1994.
These prints are part of the story of Gloria Lyon, who narrowly es-
caped death in the gas chambers at Auschwitz. Previously published in
Light in the Shadows, by Barbara Milman (Jonathan David Publishers,
Inc.)

Figure 2.8   *Madonna and Child*   Denise Satter. 16 x 20" Acrylic on
canvas, 1999.
This a painting that depicts cultural amnesia. It is a reminder that Christ
and his mother, Mary, were Jewish, and therefore would have been
incarcerated in a concentration camp and killed if they had been born
during that period of history. To the editor it reinforces the sanctity of
the mother-child bond and the pain of separation and loss experienced
in the Holocaust by both mothers and children.

Figure 2.9   *Maya II*   Chandra Garsson. 33 x 20" Mixed media and
oil on cupboard door, 1990.
The Sanskrit word for both "world" and "illusion" is *Maya*. A mask, a
doll, and written reference within the work allude not so much to the
world itself as to the filter of our individual and collective minds. The
Madonna and Child promises caring and compassion, though throughout history since birth of Christ something quite different was delivered. Very often this sanctified the mindset that made the Holocaust
possible.

Figure 2.10   *Star of David*   Chaim Goldberg. Wash & ink, 6 x 7 ½ ",
G-52,27. 1952.
Collection of the Spertus Judaica Museum, Chicago, IL.
A view of the faces and the despair in the streets of the Warsaw Ghetto,
executed from hauntings. Photo: Tommy Morgeson.

Figure 3.1 *Die Plage* (section 2) Harley Gaber. 20 x 30" Photo-collages mounted on stretched canvas. These are excerpts from approximately 5,000 canvases. The work covers the period of German history from WWI to the end of WWII. See www.dieplage.com for further description of this project.

Figure 3.2 *They Say I Have Her Bones* Deborah Trilling. 16 x 20" Oil and acrylic diptych on panel, 1995.
This portrait is based on one of the few surviving photos of Raisa. The text over the skull is a partial telling of Lillian Trilling's story. Against Raisa's wish to keep the family together, Anatole, Lillian's father, insisted that their twelve-year-old girl flee the ghetto.

Figure 3.3 *Woman in the Window* Sherry Karver. 38 x 29" Oil and computer manipulated photo images on wood, 1996. Taken from an old photograph of the artist's mother.

Figure 3.4 *1939-1945* Chaim Goldberg. Oil painting on canvas then mounted on wood. A six-panel painting, (each panel measures 70" x 32") with combined measurements of 16 feet x 70" high, G-90.32. Collection of the artist. (Individual panel titles: "Warsaw Ghetto Uprising – 1943," "Final Goodbye," "No Answer," "Trains," "Prayer," "Resistance"). 1985-1990.
Six panels that commemorate the six million Jews who perished in the Holocaust and memorialize through symbolism and representation the heroism of such situations as; the Warsaw Ghetto Uprising in 1943 and the fighting spirit that gave birth to the State of Israel, Janush Kortchak the orphanage care-taker who refused to be separated from his children, the burning of the synagogue full of praying Jews and their voices reaching for Heaven. Finally, the death-bound populations and the trains that moved them to the extermination camps, the prayers and the fighters carrying on their persistent struggle. Photos: Shalom Goldberg.

Figure 3.5 *Contemporary Ruins VIII* Judy Herzl. 22 ¾ x 23 ½ x 2 ½" Mixed media and photo, 1990.
Explores the notion that we value civilizations once they are ruins and we can display their artifacts (in museums), but rarely are able to intercede and stop the cause of the "ruining."

Figure 3.6 *My Holy Family* Deborah Trilling. 60 x 46 x 6" Mixed media (concrete, fiber, resin, paint, wood), 1993. Photo: Wilson Graham

This is a Holocaust memorial. Unlike many abstract memorials, this image reflects the tangible reality of daily life and relationships. The threesome refers to the silence of the Catholic Church during the genocide.

Figure 3.7 *Yellow Star* Deborah Trilling. 66 x 28 x 6 Mixed media (concrete, resin, silver, acrylic, wood, fiber), 1993.

This piece is the first representation of Raisa, the artist's grandmother, murdered in Treblinka. Here is her ghost as she entered Deborah's studio, frozen like a Greek tableau, yet full of life and energy. Photo: Ben Blackwell

Figure 3.*8* *Auschwitz 10* Barbara Milman. 12 x 6" Linocut, 1994.

These prints, are part of the story of Gloria Lyon, who narrowly escaped death in the gas chambers at Auschwitz. Previously published in *Light in the Shadows*, by Barbara Milman (Jonathan David Publishers, Inc.)

Figure 3.9 *I Question* Judy Herzl. 15 ¾ x 20 ½ x 5" Mixed media, photo, cedar, 1990.

Explores the concept of the witness as well as of conscience—the notion of the forest as a kind of enclave of witnesses, whether in the human sense or not.

Figure 3.10 *Foot of a Refugee* Judy Herzl. 16 x 18 x 3", Wood plaster, paint, earth, 1994.

These pieces (including *Untitled*) consider memory as the physical fragments of life as we once knew it, and also use feet as a metaphor for roots to new identities and vessels of old histories.

Figure 3.11 *Untitled* (detail) Judy Herzl. *Untitled* (detail) 13 x 18 x 72", wood, earth, Van Dyke prints on fabric, acrylic, hair.

Figure 3.12 *Prophetic Vision* 1995 Sherry Karver. 38 x 51' Oil and computer manipulated photo images on wood, 1995.
Karver has worked in the themes of memory, history and survival. Recurring images are railroad tracks which represent her parents' escape by train as well as death trains, and tornadoes, seen as an uncontrolled force and represents the chaos and turbulence of society during the Holocaust.

Figure 3.13 *Conflagration* Barbara Milman. 54 x42 x 1 ¾" Mixed media, 1993.
The woman in this piece is trapped between the flames and the string net barrier separating her from the outside world.

Figure 3.14 *Schmuckstück/Schmeckstück* (Garbage/Jewel) Deborah Trilling. 37 x 19 x 10" Mixed media (concrete, resin, pearls, wood, fiber, ink), 1994. When the women in death camps realized that they were going to be killed, they lost control of their bowels. Despite the degradation of her death, a kind of beauty is visible in this reference to Raisa before her murder. Photo: Wilson Graham

Figure 3.15 *Shtetl Nostalgia* (detail) Barbara Milman. 22 x 30 x4" Mixed media, 1998.
This piece was part of an installation titled *The Nostalgia Factory*. It contrasts sentimental idealizations of Jewish life in the small towns (shtetls) of Russia before WW II (outside panels) with the reality of life in those shtetls (inside). Photo: Greg Kinder

Figure 3.16 *Sharing Survivors* Wolf Kahn. 16 ½ x 8 x 2" Cast bronze, 1985.
This sculpture depicts survivors emerging from the rubble of liberation as they huddle together to keep warm under a blanket.

Figure 3.17 *The Black Sun* Chaim Goldberg. 29 x 36" G-60.83, Oil painting on canvas, 1960. Collection of the Spertus Judaica Museum, Chicago, IL. Photo: Shalom Goldberg.
The despicable horror that caused the sun to eclipse itself in sight of all the mass killing.

Figure 3.18 *Souvenirs* Sherry Karver. 44 x 37 x 4" Ceramic wall sculpture with wood frame, 1993

Figure 3.19 *The Final Solution Arbeit Macht Frei XVII* Harold Lewis. 26 x 17 x 20" Metal vise, inauthentic torah, wood, 1993.
Lucy Dawidowics' "What is the Use of Jewish History?" referred to the Jews as being caught in a vise. From this, it was a small leap of the imagination to conceive of this sculpture, in their words, as The Final Solution.

Figure 3.20 *Gifts from the Air* Leah Korican. 30 x 24" Oils and mixed media on canvas, 1994. Collection of Andreas Jones.
The text reads, "by night, by day, everywhere gifts from the air." It is about being grateful for our very existence and the continuity of life despite the darkness in the world and our hearts. Photos of Korican's work: Kate Cameron

Figure 3.21 *Adam & Eve* Irv Wieder. 3 x 8' Front and back of door. Mahogany.
In Irv Wieder's own words; "Door sculpture is Western Yin Yang plus human form. Organic form is not enough to overcome the minimalization and technological mechanization of our present world. (it) is symbolic of entrance and exit, beginning and end, birth and death, life's ongoing change. It represents the next step of our journey; commitment, responsibility, understanding, continually renewed by creativity..." He had developed a therapy based on the acceptance of male and female energy in each of us. This understanding is expressed in this sculpture of the icons of the original male and female.

Figure 3.22 *Remembrance* Lisa Kokin. Mixed media installation. Dimensions variable. Gut, ink, dirt, wire, stitching, 1990. Collection of the Buchenwald Memorial, Weimar-Buchenwald, Germany.
After seeing a concentration camp jacket at the Judah Magnes Museum, Lisa made this installation of ten jackets and ten bags made of hog gut, dirt and ink.

Figure 3.23 *Message 1943* Chaim Goldberg. 47 x 27 x 31" G-84.31. Aggregated colored concrete, Collection of the artist. The artist expresses the range of emotions and the voices to the horrors of the Holocaust. Message 1943 was completed in 1990, however we should note that it began as drawings that were done initially in 1944 while in Siberia and he returned to the current shape in drawing studies done in 1984, or forty years later. Photo: Shalom Goldberg.

Figure 3.24 *The Soldier and the Survivor* Wolf Kahn. 16 ½ x 5 x 2" Cast bronze, 1983.
A U.S. infantryman is stunned to witness the atrocities at a liberated concentration camp and carries a man, barely alive to a field hospital.

Figure 4.1 *Girl Alone/House Alone* Cynthia Moskowitz Brody 24 x 30" Photo collage and oils, 1984.
A representation of the sadness and loneliness of growing up in the shadow of the Holocaust and being unable to discuss it with others.

Figure 4.2 *Smoke and Memory* (closed) Cynthia Moskowitz Brody. 45 x 21 x 9 ½" Mixed media, 2000.
This most recent piece represents the women's barracks at Auschwitz. Brody found it too disturbing to use archival photographs for the women in the building, so she computer altered artistic nude photos, removing hair and making bodies more skeletal. She machine sanded a new cabinet and added broken glass and elements resembling barbed wire, though real wire would have been too threatening to deal with psychologically. When one looks at the mirrored door one's own face appears behind the fencing. Finally she felt compelled to add the actual photos of her great-grandmother, her grandmother and aunts as children as they rise in smoke above. Painful as this was, without this dose of reality she felt the piece was too sanitized, somehow dishonest. When she finally hung the heavy piece, it immediately crashed to the ground, permanently altered, as if needing to go through its own trauma to be authentic.

Figure 4.3 *Smoke and Memory* (open) Cynthia Moskowitz Brody. (see above)

Figure 4.4   *Six Million Voices Call to Me "Never Forget"* Cynthia Moskowitz Brody . 40 x 46 ½" Mixed media, 1991.
This was the first of the Holocaust-related pieces for Brody. She was afraid to take on the subject, although she felt somehow responsible to do so throughout her life. It is a self-portrait of sorts. At a distance the world seems quite beautiful with lush green forest and gold details. Upon closer inspection one will see that the beauty is haunted with images of children reaching from the limbs of trees, faces of rabbis in the grass, women in the leaves. The photo imagery was taken from Roman Vishniac's *A Vanished World*, (with permission) altered and reproduced by copy machine. The piece represents both Brody's spiritual connection to nature and the constant reminder of those who perished.

Figure 4.5   *And We Never Even Know We Have the Key* Cynthia Moskowitz Brody. 23 ½ x 24 ½ x 61 ½" Mixed media, 1998.
Although the woman locked inside the box seems trapped, she is able to make contact with the key to her freedom when the door closes if she only reaches for it. The door represents the beauty and spirituality of nature and the piece implies that we can transcend our deep sadness if we turn to something greater than ourselves.

Figure 4.6   *Family Tree* Cynthia Moskowitz Brody. 30 x 37" Photocollage and oils, 1988.
This piece is about our inability to escape our families. In the doorway the figures represent the family with which we live as adults with our own children. To the right side of the house are the original family members, our parents and siblings, still attached. In the attic window is the family secret, and growing in the trees are the ancestors, their influence ever-present. The faces, though ghostly looking, are photos of actors in drama masks. This piece was completed as she began her work as a family therapist.

Figure 4.7   *Only in Dreams* Cynthia Moskowitz Brody. 27 ½ x 38" Photo collage and oils, 1998.
This piece portrays what it feels like to inherit the fear that the world is a dangerous place and simultaneously dream of safety and comfort.

Figure 4.8 *Devotion to God* Cynthia Moskowitz Brody. 31 ½ x 25" Mixed media, 1996.
In this piece, Brody chose to represent the world of her grandfather in Eastern Europe. With found images used out of context she presents a simple man doing his work with his mind on God. The frame is covered in photocopied prayers about devotion to God. They are torn and charred to represent the history of persecution and burning of temples and the attempt to destroy a people. All Photos for Cynthia Brody: Jay Daniel

Figure 4.9 *Doublethink* Chandra Garsson. 8' x 8' Mixed media and oil on canvas back, 1989.
The caged bird is a metaphor for each human being's encasement in her own body, family, destiny, fate, and death. The tormenting question of life regarding the Holocaust becomes—"What is it to be human?" In victims and perpetrators, Garsson questions the potential to become cold and unfeeling or a victim of this mindset.

Figure 4.10 *Die Plage* (Section 2) Harley Gaber. (fig. 3.1 for details)

Figure 4.11 *Shower* Marcia Annenberg . 44 x 56 Acrylic and showerhead, 1992.
Questions the presumed absence of G-d at the time of the Holocaust. Based on Michelangelo's *Creation of Adam*, a work that testifies to an age of faith, this work conveys theological doubt as two hands reach across the gas chamber.

Figure 4.12 *Transport* Lisa Kokin. 18 x 3'x 1' Iron, wood paint, ashes, 1990.
The viewer who walks alongside Transport reads the following text on the metal plates which is taken from a newspaper article in 1990 quoting Lech Walesa who denied in a recent interview that Poles are anti-Semitic:

"Sometimes it is Jews who create an anti-Semitic atmosphere, in order to get into the limelight because on the wave of these 'anti' feelings, you can rise in position."

"There isn't anti-Semitism here in Poland," he said. "It's just called that at some moments."

Figure 4.13 *Babi Yar/Bosnia* Marcia Annenberg. 32 x 64 Acrylic on canvas, 1992.
Influenced by a painting by Andy Warhol called *Before and After*. Although his painting refers to our perception of beauty, Annenberg's painting deals with the dangers of racial stereotyping and subsequent violence.

Figure 4.14 *Man in Striped Pants* Barbara Leventhal-Stern. 3' x 3' Oil on canvas, 1995.
An homage to all of the Jewish men put into the camps. The pig in the painting stands for the lowest form of behavior, the Nazis. The pear is a symbol of the sweetness of life and earth's bounty: a sign of hope in the face of absurdity. All photos of Leventhal-Stern's work: Chris Wisner

Figure 4.15 *Hold On* Chandra Garsson. 5' x 3.5' Oil on canvas, 1991.
The spirit and body of one who endures the Nazi persecution and mass murder is dragged down to the murky depths, or else is saved, uplifted, rescued and pulled up from the drowning. It is the ambiguity itself which disturbs. It is the torture for the skinless artist or scholar who renders herself capable of knowing and feeling.

Figure 4.16 *Many Ways to Tell the Story* Cynthia Moskowitz Brody. 31 1/4 x 34" Mixed media, 1999.
There was only one photograph of Cynthia's father's family (Moskowitz) still intact before the Holocaust destroyed them. This piece utilizes that image which has been manipulated in several ways by computer, each variation representing a different facet of the impact of the loss. Family members are ghosted and placed in front of a house that is the central figure of another painting, *Family Tree*. It is framed in an actual copper roof which came from veterans housing from WW II in Massachusetts.

Figure 4.17 *We Dance* Chaim Goldberg. 72' X 30, G-86.28. Oil painting on canvas, then mounted on wood panel, 1986. Collection of the artist.
The human spirit soars in happiness as boundless love supports its eternity. Photo: Shalom Goldberg

Figure 5.1   *Resistance*   Marcia Annenberg. 32 x 44 Acrylic on canvas, 1992.
This painting is based both on a painting by Goya, *The Executions of the Third of May, 1814* , and on a photo taken in the Warsaw Ghetto. Goya's composition is updated with Nazi helmets instead of Napoleon's army uniforms. The background mirrors Goya's to show the continuity of man's suffering.

Figure 5.2   *Auschwitz Arbeit Macht Frei IV*   Harold Lewis. 16 x2 2 ½ x 15 ½" Mixed media, 1990.
Based upon a visit to the Warsaw Ghetto and the concentration camp at Auschwitz, Poland, this sculpture was the catalyst that resulted in the ten-year long creation of a series of thirty-two sculptures directly related to the Holocaust. Shown are the ever-present barbed wire, the watchtowers, barracks, gas chambers and crematoria. (All in the collection of The Holocaust and Educational Center of Nassau County, Glen Cove, N.Y.)

Figure 5.3   *Maya I*   Chandra Garsson. 33 x 20" Mixed media and oil on cupboard door, 1990.
Seemingly trapped in the box of our lives, work, the world, our bodies, *Maya* is our identification with all of this rather than our own true self. This piece portrays how each of us is trapped within his/her own personal history as well as the political history of the times we live in.

Figure 5.4   *Goebbel Prize Winner Arbeit Macht Frei VII*   Harold Lewis. 26 x14 ½ x 11" Mixed media, 1991.
During the Persian Gulf War, Iraq retaliated by unleashing Scud missile attacks on innocent women and children of Israel, who as partial protection, lived in underground shelters and were issued gas masks. The incorporation of Nazi-related photos in the mask symbolizes the ongoing anti-Semitism a half century later.

Figure 5.5   *The Warsaw Ghetto*   Barbara Milman . 78 x1 20" Oil on canvas, 1990.
Specific images were suggested by diaries and books about the Warsaw and Lodz Ghettos.

Figure 5.6   *Die Plage* (Section 2)   Harley Gaber. (see fig. 3.1 for details)

Figure 5.7   *Song Of Atonement*   Rosa Naparstek. 22 x 20 x 9" Mixed media with text, 1994.
This piece is about survivor guilt for not having been "at one" with those that perished, and the attempt to reach equilibrium with one's self and the "other" at a deeper level.

Figure 5.8   *Survivor*   Elly Simmons. 22 ½ x 30" Casein and gouache 1995.
A camp survivor standing amidst the flames of the Shoah, a fascist Nazi dog threatening her calm. Dark clouds of ash surround her, she wears the camp uniform but stands strong and calm in the midst of hell. She resembles a composite of four great aunts who were all shot in one day by Germans who marched into Lvov, Russia. Elly would have had many family members had Betye, Elena, Dora and Rebecca survived.

Figure 5.9   *My Trip to Buchenwald #1* (detail)   Lisa Kokin.. 125 x 22" Gut, found objects, barbed wire, imitation sinew, 1996.
In 1996 Lisa was invited to supervise the installation of *Remembrance* as part of the permanent collection of the Buchenwald Memorial. The museum on the site of the camp contained a glass vitrine with hundreds of buttons, eyeglass fragments, and other tiny items collected on the grounds after the war, everyday objects which were all that remained of thousands of vanished lives. When she returned from her trip she made a series of pieces using gut and found objects, of which *My Trip to Buchenwald #1* is part.

Figure 5.10   *Dybbuk*   Elly Simmons. 32 x 40" Pastel on Rag, 1988.
"The Dybbuk" was an image commissioned by A Traveling Jewish Theater for their 10th anniversary production of the classic 1920s play "The Dybbuk" written by Saul Ansky. It is based on a 16th century Jewish ghost story, a story of possession and exorcism which foretold the turmoil and massive changes sweeping Jewish culture and all of the world in the first half of the 20th century, leading up to the destruction of the Second World War. This piece has also been woven into a 5 'x 7' tapestry.

Figure 6.1 *Captives* Dorrit Title. 30 x 22" Monotype, 1986.
Captives echoes art works depicting Adam and Eve on side panels. The
two standing figures become symbols of the original man and woman,
representing the millions who died in the Holocaust as prisoners in
the Nazi camps. She chose Monotype, a form of printmaking that lends
itself to spontaneous line with only one print, to express strong emotional impact.

Figure 6.2 *Memorial* Dorrit Title. 65 x 36" Mixed Media construction, 1986.
The portraits in "Memorial" were inspired by photos of Jewish victims
of the Nazis. They represent the millions whose faces we do not know.
Through art Dorrit sought to give them identity. *Yahrzeit* (memorial)
candles burn in their memory at the base of the construction on which
the names of concentration camps are inscribed.

Figure 6.3 *Wedding Party 1941* Marcia Annenberg. 40 x 56 Acrylic
on canvas, 1992.
Captures a moment poised on the threshold of disaster. The painting
is based on a family photograph. The yellow stars, however, indicate
that the entire family most likely perished.

Figure 6.4 *Listen to the Flames* Toan Klein. 20 x 58 x 22" Gatographs
(patented) encased photos in glass, optical glass, sandblasting, dalle
du verre, hot tooled glass, acrylic wicks, silicone and blown glass.
This piece won a gold award in the international competition, Artists
Confronting the Inconceivable. The candles are placed in rows of seven
(days) and twelve (months) to symbolize the time these people lost.
The central candle, or *shamas*, shows a picture loaned by Yad Vashem
in Jerusalem. Through the shamas can be seen a *yahrzeit* lamp which
burns for eighteen hours. In Hebrew, the word for eighteen - *chai* - is
also the word for "life." Scattered around the memorial are shards of
glass in remembrance of Kristallnacht. Each chip has been etched with
the words "the children" in a different language.

Figure 6.5   *No Killing*   Deborah Trilling. 10 x 10 x 5" Mixed media (oil on panel, concrete, fiber, resin, gold leaf, wax, ink), 1993.
This portrait of Raisa is akin to Retablo altars and Byzantine icons, both of which establish links between the viewer and the realm of the divine inhabited by the subject. Photo: Ben Blackwell

Figure 6.6   *Klezmer Dreams*   Lauren Herzog Schwartz. 24 x 29" Monotype, 1990.
Through color, gesture, and movement, Lauren tried to capture the beauty and joy of the Old Country, during a time of innocence. As she made this piece, she could almost feel the music and dance of a place she can only imagine. Lauren's work has been informed by her experience as the daughter of a woman who escaped from Prague in November 1939, made it to the U.S. to attend college, but lost the majority of her family. Lauren's art has served as a bridge, enabling mother and daughter to communicate and come to terms with the past.

Figure 6.7   *Angel of the Light*   Denise Satter. 18 x 24" Acrylic on canvas, 1992.
Although somewhat bleak, this painting is actually one of hope. In this case, hope being the lineage of Jews that survived the camps remained unbroken to become the children of survivors, such as myself. The little lights in the tree symbolize these children. However, the graveyard, based on the Jewish graveyard in Prague, Czech Republic, symbolizes the deaths of many, as do the clouds billowing from the gas ovens in the background.

Figure 6.8   *The Last Way*   Chaim Goldberg. 38 x 51" G-60.02 Painting on linen, 1960.
Collection of Spertus Judaica Museum, Chicago, IL. Photo by Shalom Goldberg.
A somber, gray day, depicts the death march that emptied the Jewish population from the smallest of the shtetls and its surrounding areas.

Figure 6.9   *Ode to Joy*   Chaim Goldberg. 9' x 28" x 27" G-82.74.
Wood carving from one trunk of an oak tree, 1982. Collection of the
artist. Photo by Shalom Goldberg.
A wood carving that celebrates the triumph of the human spirit.

Figure 6.10   *My Mother, My Daughter—a Tree of Life*   Elly Simmons.
31 ½ x 24" Casein and collage, 1993.
Created in 1993 soon after the birth of her daughter Maralisa, it reflects the eternal cycle of life, particularly of the Motherline, the continuity of life from grandmother to mother, to self, to daughter and on
and on and on. Her daughter as an infant floats suspended in a great
sun, bursting into life at the top of a great tree of life, also a menorah
lit with flaming candles. Her mother, as a young woman, stands rooted
at the bottom of this symbol of growth. A sea of flames licks at the
base of the blazing menorah. This image springs from the master Uru-
guayan writer Eduardo Galeano's story in *The Book of Embraces*.

Index

265

Biographical Notes

Artists

Marcia Annenberg

Born in New York City with familial roots in Russia, Hungary and Lithuania, Marcia Annenberg has had solo shows at the Holocaust Memorial Resource and Education Center of Central Florida and the Rockland Center for Holocaust Studies in New York. Her work was recently exhibited in a show at the Red Chair Gallery in Missouri entitled, "Tackling Meaning: The Curators Playbook." The Butler Institute of American Art included a painting in its 61st Annual Midyear Exhibition. She has had several venues in Soho including the Limner Gallery's Highlights '93, The Westbroadway Gallery, The 55 Mercer Street Gallery and the National Arts Club in Gramercy Park. In April 2001, her work will be on view at the New Century Artists Gallery in New York City.

Cynthia Moskowitz Brody

Contributing editor of *Bittersweet Legacy–Creative Responses to the Holocaust*, Cynthia Moskowitz Brody is the child of two Holocaust survivors. Her mother lived through six months in Auschwitz in addition to two other camps, and her father survived much trauma as a forced laborer in Russia. Eighty-six members of her family died at Auschwitz. That legacy of sadness and survival has also fueled the fervent desire to create change through her work. She has been an exhibiting mixed media artist for over 25 years and co-curated the first public exhibition of work based on this anthology at the Triton Museum of Art in Santa Clara, California in January 2000. She also writes poetry and is a licensed Marriage & Family Therapist in the San Francisco Bay area. She has passed on this bittersweet legacy to her daughter, Julie and son, Jonathan.

Harley Gaber

Harley Gaber was born in 1943 and has spent the past forty years involved in music, photography and art. Included are excerpts from approximately 5,000 canvases covering the period of German history from WWI to the end of WWII. See www.dieplage.com for further description of this project.

Chandra Garsson

Chandra Garsson was born in 1954 in Los Angeles, California. Her family is Jewish and all four grandparents came to the United States to escape the pogroms in their Eastern European homeland. If they had not come to this country they might have perished along with the rest. She received an art degree from University of California at Santa Cruz and Masters of Fine Art degree from San Jose State University in 1987. Exhibitions have included the Jewish Museum in San Francisco, the Oakland Museum and the Triton Museum in Santa Clara, CA. Her work has also been shown in New Zealand and Singapore.

Chaim Goldberg

The ninth of eleven children, Chaim Goldberg was Born on March 20, 1917 in the Shtetl Kazimierz Dolny in Poland. Chaim Goldberg knew from a very early age that his passion for making art was to become his whole life. He loved his small village and its simple ways, its unique Jewish way of life and its people. Combined with the great pain and loss of that whole era became the two most moving themes in his art. His artistic talents were discovered at the age of fourteen by a traveler to the village who obtained scholarships for the young protégé and helped in making it possible for him to attend the High School for Fine Arts in Krakow and later the Academy of Fine Arts in Warsaw.

The Holocaust changed his life forever. Goldberg managed to escape a POW camp and other devastation and along with his future wife became refugees in Siberia. He designed sets for the Novosibirsk Opera house and worked as an artist as well as labor as was needed. After the war Goldberg attended the Ecole de Beaux Art in Paris and in 1955 was able to immigrate to Israel. In 1967, he and his family arrived in New York for an exhibition tour that led to becoming a citizen. His works are included in such prestigious collections as the Metropolitan Museum of Art in New York, Smithsonian Institution, Spertus Judaica Museum in Chicago, Judah Magnes Museum in San Francisco, the Houston Museum of Fine Art and many others the world over. Goldberg's art celebrates the dignity and nobility of mankind in all his themes.

Judy Herzl

Judy Herzl works in mixed media, photography, sculpture and installation. Her work is often concerned with issues of humanity and conscience, motivated in part by being a first generation American and a child of Holocaust survivors. Her newest work comes out of her experiences while in a solitary Buddhist retreat and reflects emptiness and the separation of self and "other." Her work has been featured in over forty solo and group exhibitions in such institutions as The Soros Center and Artists House in the Ukraine, The Jewish Museum-San Francisco, The Museum of New Mexico, Santa Fe, NM, and the The Cheekwood Museum of Art, Nashville, TN. In 1987 she was the first recipient of the Willard Van Dyke Memorial Grant sponsored by the New Mexico Council on Photography.

Wolf Kahn

Wolf Kahn was born in Ludwigshaven, Germany, and narrowly escaped to the U.S. with his parents and two brothers. He served with distinction in the U.S. Army Air Corps where he taught German to judge advocates who were prosecuting Nazi leaders in Nuremberg. He has received numerous national and international awards for his achievements in various media.

Sherry Karver

Sherry Karver was born and raised in Chicago, IL, a child of Holocaust survivors. She attended the Art Institute of Chicago and Indiana University, where she received a B.A. degree in sociology. She later attended Tulane University in New Orleans, LA where she received a M.F.A. in ceramics. She was a ceramic sculptor until 1995 when she made a major change to oil painting, incorporating photo images and computer manipulation. She has worked in the themes of memory, history and survival. Recurring images are railroad tracks which represent her parents' escape by train as well as death trains, and tornadoes, seen as an uncontrolled force and represents the chaos and turbulence of society during the Holocaust. Sherry Karver's work is represented by LewAllen Contemporary Gallery, Santa Fe, Lisa Harris Gallery, Seattle, and Olga Dollar Gallery, San Francisco.

Toan Klein

Nineteen people in Toan Klein's family, all Lithuanian Jews from the villages of Vishtinetz, Naishtut-Shaki, Vilkovishk and Kovno, were killed during the Holocaust. Toan's mother and her immediate family, through a series of lucky events, left Lithuania before the war broke out. Virtually all the relatives they left behind, including his greatgrandparents, were killed. This is the only memorial that exists to record their lives and deaths. In "Listen to the Flames," Toan has tried to go beyond the general to the specific, and to make something beautiful and alive out of something horrible and deadly.

Lisa Kokin

Lisa Kokin has exhibited her artist's books, sculpture and installation nationally and internationally. She has been the recipient of numerous awards, including a WESTAF/NEA Regional Fellowship (1995), a California Arts Council Visual Arts Fellowship (1998) and a Eureka Fellowship (1998). Her work is in private and public collections, including the Buchenwald Memorial in Weimar-Buchenwald, Germany. Ms. Kokin's work deals with themes of personal history and social commentary through the use of found materials. She is represented by the Catharine Clark Gallery in San Francisco.

Despite the fact that Kokin's family was not directly affected by the Holocaust, it cast a shadow over her childhood and had a significant effect on her world view. As a child attending Hebrew school, she was shown films containing graphic scenes from the death camps which were meant to teach her about what it meant to be a Jew. Her response was to turn away from everything Jewish for the next twenty-five years. In 1990 while visiting the Judah Magnes Museum in Berkeley, California, she saw a concentration camp jacket and realized it was time to look at her relationship to the Holocaust, this time as an adult and voluntarily. Since that time she has created a series of books, sculptures and installations on the Holocaust, anti-Semitism and related themes.

Leah Korican

Leah Korican's mother is from Poland and her father is from Yugoslavia. Her mother escaped Europe during WW II with her parents and sister and came to the United States via Belgium, Spain, and Portugal. Her mother's extended family in Krakow perished. Her father and his family fled to Italy where they were hidden and saved by families in a small village outside of Florence. Her grandfather was arrested and interned in Yugoslavia. He was shot, just weeks before the war's end, after escaping from a camp. Eventually her father and his mother immigrated to New York. In the summer of 1999, Leah, along with her sister, father, and cousins, went back to Quarata, the village where her father's family had hidden. She saw the hiding places and thanked the children of the families who hid them. Here was horror and beauty, loss and gift. Currently Leah lives in Oakland, California where she works as a visual artist, poet, and teacher.

Barbara Leventhal-Stern

Barbara Leventhal-Stern was born in Springfield, Ohio. Her grandparents are from Russia, Poland and Hungary. She has always been interested in her eastern European legacy and has been haunted by the Holocaust since she was in her teens. She began her art training in Washington University School of Fine Art in St. Louis, Missouri. She received her B.F.A. from The Boston Museum School and Tufts University. She taught art for the Workers Educational Association in Cambridge, England, and studied graphics at The London Polytech. She began her graduate work at The Claremont Graduate School of Art, and was awarded a Masters Degree in printmaking from San Jose State University in 1985, and is also a licensed Marriage & Family Therapist.

Harold Lewis

Harold Lewis was born in 1913 on the Lower East Side of New York, the youngest of seven children of penniless immigrants from Poland. He studied and obtained BS and MA degrees while raising a family of three daughters and spent forty-three years as director of a nursery school and children's summer day camp. At age sixty he retired and began a second career as a sculptor. During the next twenty-one years he created nearly 200 pieces of sculpture and was awarded prizes as well as exhibiting in one and two person shows. Now, retired at age eighty-six with his wife, Adina, he resides at a retirement community in Canton, Massachusetts.

Barbara Milman

Starting with a series of paintings in 1990, much of Barbara Milman's work has been about the Holocaust. In 1997 Jonathan David Publishers released a book of her linoleum prints, *Light in the Shadows*, based on interviews she conducted with Holocaust survivors. She continued to concentrate on printmaking, and in 1999 she was awarded a printmaking fellowship at the Kala Institute in Berkeley, California. Where she is presently an artist-in-residence. Her work addresses the Holocaust and its relationship to other events of the twentieth century. Barbara Milman is a member of the California Society of Printmakers, the National Association of Women Artists, and the Women's Caucus for Art. She has had over 30 solo shows throughout the United States, and has been included in over 200 group shows throughout the country. Her art can be found in many public and museum collections, including The Art Museum at Yad Vashem, Jerusalem, Israel, and the National Women Artists' Collection at the Zimmerli Museum at Rutgers University. Her work is also included in *The Best of Printmaking: An International Collection* (1997).

Rosa Naparstek

Rosa Naparstek went to college to study physics hoping that by understanding the fundamental elements of the universe she would understand the world. Finding the approach too mechanistic, she searched for answers in many other disciplines. As a student, she was a political activist and later became an attorney in furtherance of her commitment to social and political change. After practicing law for several years, she realized that fundamental political change could not occur without personal transformation. This shift in perspective challenged her to look inside for the emotional roots of the world we create personally and politically. Much of what she does centers around childhood memories and experiences and is concerned with questions of cruelty and its source within us. Rosa believes the fundamental human questions are about good and evil and that each person, culture, and even each civilization asks these through the lens of its own experience. Hers was the Holocaust.

Lauren Herzog Schwartz

Lauren Herzog Schwartz is a California artist who works in various media including drawing, painting and printmaking. Her work has appeared in Bay Area shows and galleries. She began studying fine arts in her late twenties as a way to learn more about herself, and continues to explore how the process of creating art can be transformative for individuals and groups.

Elly Simmons

Over the last five years Elly Simmons has organized and exhibited work in the "No More Scapegoats" exhibit shown in conjunction with "Anne Frank in the World Today", an historic traveling exhibition examining the roots of prejudice and the conditions which led to the rise of Nazism and the Holocaust. "No More Scapegoats" connects the life and times of Anne Frank with our challenge to confront racism and intolerance today.

Sharon Siskin

Sharon Siskin is a nationally exhibiting artist, art teacher and community art activist. Her work has been exhibited in many museums including The Jewish Museum and M. H. de Young Memorial Museum in San Francisco, the Oakland Museum, and the alternative Museum in New York. Her artwork is featured in *Connecting Conversations: Interviews with 28 Bay Area Women Artists*, Moira Roth, editor; *Site to Sight: Mapping Bay Area Visual Culture*, Lydia Matthiews, editor, as well as other publications. She is the recipient of ten California Arts Council Artist in Residence grants as well as dozens of public art funds and private foundations and she also started Positive Art in 1988. It is a project which provides opportunities to artists and students living with AIDS/HIV.

Denise Satter

Over the past twenty years she has illustrated a wide variety of book covers, book interiors, textbooks, magazine articles, greeting cards and stationery products, children's album covers, advertisements and textile designs. As a freelance artist she has exhibited in many galleries and museum shows across the country. Her work is included in many private and corporate collections, including Johnson and Johnson and Nabisco. She received a grant from the New Jersey State Council on the Arts to complete a children's environmental book and is currently working on one about cats. In 1989 she won New Jersey State Council on the Arts Grant for Graphic Arts. She curated and exhibited in the "Ancient Myths and Modern Urban Legends" show at Galeria Tonantzin, San Juan Baptista, California. Denise co-curated and exhibited her work in the first museum exhibit derived from this anthology, "Bittersweet Legacy - Creative Responses to the Holocaust" at The Triton Museum, Santa Clara, CA in January 2000.

Dorrit Title

Dorrit Title was born in Vienna in 1937. At the age of two, she fled the Nazis with her parents and came to New York. Her grandparents and other family members tried in vain to emigrate, but were denied visas and died in extermination camps. Art is her form of communicating the tragedy of the Holocaust to present and future generations with the hope that through understanding, our world can achieve tolerance and prevent the recurrence of genocide. She is a graduate of The Cooper Union Art School and the San Francisco Art Institute. She has had solo shows at The Holocaust Memorial and Educational Center of Nassau County (1997), Temple Judea of Manhasset (1996), and The Rockland Center for Holocaust Studies (1991). She has also exhibited at many other museums and galleries including The Fine Arts Museum of Long Island and Queensborough Community College, where her work is in permanent collections.

Deborah Trilling

Deborah Trilling has been producing artwork since the nineteen eighties. She has degrees from Berkeley and Stanford, where she studied art with Frank Lobdell, Joel Leivick and Nathan Olivera. She has shown her work in numerous exhibitions including the Los Angeles Museum of the Holocaust. Her art is discussed in Stephen Feinstein's *Indelible Images: Contemporary Art about the Holocaust* (in press). Trilling's work evokes the absence of a missing Holocaust generation and establishes contact with the members of her family who were murdered.

Irv Wieder

Until his death, shortly before the publication of this book, Irv Wieder was an award winning artist and a therapist living and working in Santa Fe, New Mexico. He survived the Holocaust as a child and brought depth and spirituality to his community and his work. Sadly, those early experiences and memories proved too much to bear and he took his life. This publication of his work memorializes his life and honors his art. It also underscores the pain and burden which are part of the legacy of the Holocaust.

Biographical Notes

Authors

Yehuda Amichai

Yehuda Amichai (1924-2000) was Israel's leading poet and a literary figure of international stature; his work has been translated into thirty-seven languages, including Catalan, Estonian, Korean, Serbo-Croatian, and Vietnamese. Born in 1924 in Germany, he emigrated with his parents to Palestine in 1936, and lived with his wife and children in Jerusalem. Amichai is the recipient of numerous awards, including the Israel Prize, his country's highest honor. The English translation of *Open Closed Open* his magnum opus, was published by Harcourt a few months before his death.

Sari Aviv

Sari Aviv wrote "A Stab" as a freshman at Cranbrook-Kingswood High School in Bloomfield Hills, Michigan. Sari will graduate from Brown University with the class of 2001. She plans to be a journalist.

Chana Bloch

Chana Bloch, a poet, translator, scholar and literary critic, is author of three books of poems, *The Secrets of the Tribe, The Past Keeps Changing*, and *Mrs. Dumpty*, as well as translations of the biblical *Song of Songs* and the Israeli poets Yehuda Amichai (*The Selected Poetry* and *Open*

276

Closed Open) and Dahlia Ravikovitch (*A Dress of Fire* and *The Window: New and Selected Poems*). She is Professor of English and Director of the Creative Writing Program at Mills College in Oakland, California.

Cynthia Moskowitz Brody

Contributing editor of *Bittersweet Legacy–Creative Responses to the Holocaust*, Cynthia Moskowitz Brody is the child of two Holocaust survivors. Her mother lived through six months in Auschwitz as well as other camps, and her father survived much trauma as a forced laborer in Russia. Eighty-six members of her family died at Auschwitz. That legacy of sadness and survival has also carried the fervent desire to create change through her work. She has been an exhibiting mixed media artist for over 25 years, writes poetry, and is a licensed Marriage & Family Therapist in the San Francisco Bay area. She has passed on this bittersweet legacy to her daughter, Julie and son, Jonathan.

Ruth Daigon

Ruth Daigon was winner of the Ann Stanford Poetry Award, in 1997 and the "The Eve of St. Agnes" Poetry Award in 1994. Prior to her career in poetry she was a professional singer: a Columbia Recording artist, a guest artist on CBS's Camera Three, a soloist with the New York Pro Musica. In the late seventies, she made the transition to full time poet, editor, and performance artist. She was founder/editor of the poetry publication *Poets On:* for twenty years. Daigon is a regular on the Internet with 3 chapbooks on *Web Del Sol, Pares Cum Paribus* (Chile) and *The Alsop Review* plus numerous publications in hard copy magazines and anthologies. Her poetry collection, *Between One Future And The Next*, (Papier- Mache Press), was published in 1995. Her latest book, *The Moon Inside,* has just been published (Gravity/Newton's Baby). A selection of her poems entitled *Ruth Daigon's Greatest Hits* is forthcoming from Pudding House publications as part of their Gold chapbook series. Daigon recently won the Greensboro National Poetry Award. Another chapbook, *Payday At The Triangle,* is based on the terrible Triangle factory fire in New York City in 1911. Her chapbook is the winner in a contest run by Kimera and will be included in an anthology to be published in February of 2001.

Enid Dame

Enid Dame is a poet, writer, editor and teacher living in Brooklyn and High Falls, NY. Her books of poems include *Lilith and her Demons* (Cross-Cultural Communications, 1989) and *Anything You Don't See* (West End Press, 1992). She has taught creative writing at Rutgers University and is currently a lecturer at New Jersey Institute of Technology. She has given presentations of Jewish women's poetry, and led workshops on *midrash*ic writing at the Institute for Institutions. She is co-editor of the anthology, *Which Lilith? Feminist Writers Re-Create the World's First Woman* (Jason Aronson, 1998). With her husband, the poet Donald Lev, she co-edits *Home Planet News,* a literary tabloid that celebrated its 20th anniversary in March 1999. She is also a member of the Editorial Collective of *Bridges,* a Jewish feminist magazine. She has just completed a book of poetry, focusing on biblical characters, especially women, who speak in contemporary voices. She read in the Geraldine Dodge Poetry Festival this September as one of the "Poets Among Us."

Cortney Davis

Cortney Davis is the author of *Details of Flesh* (Calyx, 1997) and co-editor of *Between the Heartbeats: Poetry and Prose by Nurses* (University of Iowa, 1995). Her poems have been published in *Poetry, Witness, Ontario Review, Hudson Review*, and other journals. A non-fiction narrative about her work as a nurse practitioner in women's health is forthcoming from Random House, *I Knew a Woman: the Experience of the Female Body.*

Annie Dawid

Annie Dawid's newest book, a collection of short stories, *Lily in the Desert,* will be published in the Spring of 2001 by Carnegie-Mellon University Press. Her first book, a novel, *York Ferry,* is in a second printing from Cane Hill Press of New York. Her work has been anthologized in the *American Fiction World of Bearing Witness to the Holocaust.*

Adam D. Fisher

Adam D. Fisher has served as Rabbi of Temple Isaiah, Stony Brook, NY since 1971. His poetry has appeared in Jewish and general literary journals including: *Judaism, CCAR Journal, Long Island Quarterly, West Hills Review and Manhatten Poetry Review*. His books of poems include *Rooms, Airy Rooms*, and *Dancing Alone*. His short fiction has appeared in *The Jewish Spectator* and *Echoes*. He is the author of two books of liturgy: *Seder Tu Bishevat, The Festival of Trees*, and *An Everlasting Name, A Service for Remembering the Shoah*. His most recent book is *God's Garden*, a book of stories for children. He is married to wife Eileen and has two daughters and three grandchildren.

Charles Fishman

Charles Fishman served as director of the SUNY Farmingdale Visiting Writers Program for eighteen years and was the originator of the Paumanok Poetry Award. He has served as a poetry consultant to the U.S. Holocaust Memorial Museum in Washington, DC (1995-). His books include *Mortal Companions*, the *Firewalkers, Blood to Remember: American Poets on the Holocaust*, and *The Death Mazurka*, which was selected by the American Library Association as one of the outstanding books of the year (1989) and nominated for the 1990 Pulitzer Prize in Poetry. His poems, translations, reviews and essays have appeared in more than 300 periodicals. He has received the Ann Stanford Poetry Prize from Southern California Anthology, The Eve of St. Agnes Poetry Prize from *Negative Capability*, the Gertrude B. Claytor Memorial Award from the Poetry Society of America, and a fellowship in poetry from the New York Foundation for the Arts. He was the final judge for the 1998 Capricorn Book Award, served as Poetry Editor for both the *Journal of Genocide Research* and *Cistercian Studies Quarterly*, and is currently Associate Editor of *The Drunken Boat*, a Web-based poetry review. His next book, *Country of Memory*, will be released by Rattapallax Press in 2001.

Jacqueline Fishman

Jackie Fishman has taught high school English and Holocaust studies for twenty years and is the mother of two teens. She is the daughter of an Auschwitz survivor and feels her work is an attempt at dealing with this compelling and frightening heritage.

Harry Fiss

Harry Fiss was born in Vienna, Austria, in 1926. Shortly after the *Anschluss* (Hitler's annexation of Austria) in March 1938, Fiss, along with all the other Jewish students, was expelled from public school and deprived of education until he and his parents managed to flee to the United States late in 1939. Many of Fiss's closest friends and relatives disappeared and were never heard from again. His parents fortunately were spared, though beaten, tortured and humiliated. After his arrival in the United States, Fiss served for two years in the U.S. Army. Most of this time was spent in post-war Germany, at the International Military Tribunal in Nuremberg, where he was soon put in charge of documentation of the American Prosecutor General, Telford Taylor. It was while at Nuremberg that he experienced the confrontation with Hoess described so vividly in his poem. By profession, Fiss is a clinical psychologist who has been practicing, teaching and doing research for over forty years. He also frequently lectures on the Holocaust and Nuremberg war crimes trial.

Stewart Florsheim

Stewart Florsheim's parents are refugees from Hitler's Germany. His grandfather survived Dachau; other relatives were not as fortunate. His poetry has been widely published in small press periodicals and anthologies. His poetry appeared in *DoubleTake Magazine* (Center for Documentary Studies, Duke University, 1996), *Slipstream 19* (Slipstream Publications, 1999), *The Seattle Review* (University of Washington, 2000), and *Rattle 14* (Bombshelter Press, 2000). He is the editor of *Ghosts of the Holocaust* (Wayne State University Press, 1989), an anthology of poetry by children of Holocaust survivors. His work is included in the anthology, *Unsettling America: Race and Ethnicity in Contemporary American Poetry* (Viking Penguin, 1994) and *And What Rough Beast* (The Ashland Poetry Press, 1999) He lives in the Bay Area, where he manages technical writers for a computer software company.

Paula Naomi Friedman

Paula Naomi Friedman is an author, editor, and publicist living in Richmond, CA. She has received Pushcart Prize nominations and her stories and poems have appeared in numerous small press magazines and anthologies. She directs the Anna Davidson Rosenberg Award for Poems on the Jewish Experience and was founding editor of the *Open Cell* literary review and co-editor of the *Gathered from the Center* women's poetry anthology. She handles public relations for the Judah Magnes Museum in Berkeley, CA, and edits books for the University of California Press and others.

David Gershator

David Gershator was born on Mt. Carmel and left the mountain for N.Y. via Egypt on the first civilian ship to cross the Atlantic after WWII. Poetry publications include *Elijah's Child* (Cross Cultural Communications, 1992). His work has been featured in *Home Planet News* and has appeared in several anthologies. *New Directions* published his translation of *Federica Garcia Lorca: Selected Letters*. He co-edited *Downtown Poets Press* in N.Y. for ten years, received a N.Y. State Creative Arts Public Service Award and NEH grant, and co-authored several children's books including *Palampam Day* (Cavendish, 1997) and *Bread is For Eating* (Holt, 1995), a PBS Reading Rainbow featured selection. Gershator receiving advanced degrees at Columbia and N.Y.U. and has taught at various American universities, including the University of the Virgin Islands. He was a guest lecturer on the S.S. Rotterdam world cruise. As an artist and poet he has participated in multi-media exhibitions in N.J., N.Y. and his home island of St. Thomas.

Liselotte Erlanger Glozer

Born in Munich in 1915, Liselotte left in 1936 and came to America in 1938. She has published widely in poetry journals and little magazines. She is preparing to publish a book of short stories presently.

Beth Aviv Greenbaum

Beth Aviv Greenbaum teaches English and Holocaust Literature at Groves High School in Birmingham, Michigan. She has written a collection of short stories and a young adult novel, *Borders*.

Eva Gross

Eva Gross is a Hungarian survivor of the Holocaust, a retired teacher with an M. A. in Literature, a student of the Torah, an award winning author, poet, TV producer and painter. Seven of her books received grants for publication and are in the Skokie Public Library. She is a Skokie Fine Arts Commissioner, member of the Skokie Art Guild, co-founder of Grassfield Writers' Collective and was honored by former Governor Jim Edgar for "contributing all the talent, energy and time devoted to strengthening the cultural fabric of this great state and enriching the lives of many."

Annette Bialik Harchik

Annette Bialik Harchik is a poet, educator, and translator. Born in Europe, she is fluent in Yiddish and often uses the language in her work. Her parents, from small towns in Poland, were the sole survivors of their large families. They endured the ghettos and death camps of Aushchwitz and Dachau until their liberation by the Allies.

Her mother, Franja, after giving birth to Annette, became mentally ill and never recovered. Her body had been able to survive but not her mind or soul. This is the only one of her own poems she did not destroy:

> Hitler, I will never forget
> How you burned my mother.
> My father died in my arms.
> You herded my sisters and brother
> Into gas chambers
> And left me, as lost as a leaf from a tree
> That the wind blows far across the field.

Annette's poetry focuses on personal loss in the Holocaust, issues in Jewish identity, and the quest for selfhood. Her poems have appeared in small press magazines and the following anthologies: *Ghosts of The Holocaust*, edited by Stewart J. Florsheim, Wayne State University Press, 1989; *Sarah's Daughters Sing, A Sampler of Poems by Jewish Women*, edited by Henny Wenkart, Ktav Press, 1990; and *Blood To Remember, American Poets On The Holocaust*, edited by Charles Fishman, Texas Tech University Press, 1991. Annette resides in Manhattan with her husband and two daughters.

Roald Hoffmann

Roald Hoffmann was born in 1937 in Zloczow, then Poland, now Ukraine. After surviving the Nazi occupation he and his mother and stepfather made their way to New York City in 1949. He has degrees from Columbia University and Harvard University with a Ph.D. in Chemical Physics. He has been engaged in teaching and research in theoretical chemistry at Cornell University since 1965.

Roald Hoffmann has published many individual poems and three collections: *The Metamict State*, 1987, and *Gaps and Verges*, 1990, (University of Central Florida Press) and *Memory Effects* (Calhoun Press, 1990) Hoffmann also writes nonfiction: *Chemistry Imagined*, with artist Vivian Torrence, (Smithsonian Institution Press, 1993); *The Same and Not the Same*, (Columbia University Press, 1995) which was translated into several languages; and *Old Wine, New Flasks: Reflections on Science and Jewish Tradition*, with Shira Leibowitz Schmidt, (W.H. Freeman, 1997). A play by Carl Djerassi and Roald Hoffmann, *Oxygen*, is headed for American, British and Swedish productions in 2001.

Irena Klepfisz

Irena Klepfisz, a poet and activist, was born in Poland in 1941 and came to the U.S. at the age of eight. A recipient of an NEA poetry fellowship and translation grants, she is the author of *A Few Words in the Mother Tongue* (poetry) and *Dreams of an Insomniac* (essays) and a co-editor the *Tribe of Dina: A Jewish Woman's Anthology* and *Di froyen: Women and Yiddish*. Her scholarly work includes articles on Eastern European Jewish women activists and Yiddish women writers. Most recently she has focused much of her work on translating Yiddish women's poetry and fiction. In addition to reclamation of Yiddish and Yiddish secular culture, her activism and writing also promoted peace between Israelis and Palestinians and greater acceptance for gays and lesbians in the Jewish community. She teaches women's studies at Barnard College.

Yala Korwin

Yala Korwin, a visual artist and retired Art Librarian, is the author of the book, *To Tell the Story – Poems of the Holocaust*, distributed by the US Holocaust Memorial Museum, Washington, DC. Her poems have been published in poetry magazines and included in the following anthologies: *Beyond Lament*, ed. M. Striar, (Northwestern U Press, 1998): *Blood to Remember*, ed. Charles Fishman, (Texas Tech. Univ. Press, 1991); *Images from the Holocaust – A Literature Anthology*, ed. J. E. Brown et al., (National Textbook Co., 1997); *Voices of the Holocaust*, ed. M. McGhee et al., (National Textbook Co., 1997); *Sarah's Daughters Sing*, ed. Henny Wenkart, (KTAV Publishing House, 1990); *Anthology of Magazine Verse*, ed. A. F. Pater, (Monitor Book Co., 1986-88 & 1997); and, *Patchwork of Dreams*, ed. M.Sklar, (The Spirit That Moves Us Press, 1996).

Gabriel Ariel Levicky

Gabriel Ariel Levicky was born to a family of Shoah survivors in the former Czechoslovakia. He soon embarked on "silent" opposition, being influenced among many other impacts by the American Beat, Rock & Roll and blues music and visual arts. He organized many happenings and forbidden "Flying University" meetings, signed Charter 77 (lead by Vaclav Havel) for which he was heavily persecuted. In 1977 he published his first samizdat Neznama Poezia, *The Unknown Poetry*. In 1979 he "miraculously" escaped via 5 countries and made it into the USA. First, he settled in New York City; after a short stay there, he went to San Francisco where he published a second book, *The Unknown Poetry # 2*. He organized various poetry projects and performed at different open mike readings. Back in New York, he reestablished himself on the local poetry scene, while working on a new collection *B (lack) & W (hite) Wet Paint Poems*, encompassing his NY experience. He is also an accomplished cartoonist and visual artist.

Lyn Lifshin

Lyn Lifshin's most recent book, *Before It's Light*, was published in the winter of 2000 by Black Sparrow press, following their publication of *Cold Comfort* in 1997. She has published more than 100 books of poetry, including *Blue Tattoo*, poems of the Holocaust and *Marilyn Monroe*, and won awards for her non-fiction and edited four anthologies of women's writing, including *Tangled Vines, Ariadne's Thread*, and *Lips Unsealed*. Her poems have appeared in most literary and poetry magazines, and she is the subject of an award winning documentary film, *Lyn Lifshin: Not Made of Glass*. Her poem, "No More Apologizing", has been called "among the most impressive documents of the women's poetry movement." Lifshin has given more than 700 readings at universities, museums and libraries and has been Poet in Residence at the University of Rochester, Antioch, and Colorado Mountain College. She is the winner of numerous awards including the Jack Kerouac Award for her book *Kiss the Skin Off*.

Leatrice Lifshitz

As a young mother, Leatrice Lifshitz's overwhelming concern was how to protect her children. Where to hide them? (In the back of a closet? With a bottle of milk?) It was something that she thought about often. It became a recurring nightmare. Since then she has edited a book, *Voices: Jews in a Circle*, which attempts to define what a Jewish memory is. She has written a novel about the two apocryphal women who survived the destruction of Masada in 73 C.E., *One Crack, Two Cracks, Three Cracks, Four*, a finalist in the Willa Cather Fiction Contest, 1998, and a semi-finalist in the Heekin Group James Fellowship Contest, 1998. She has had poetry published in many poetry journals and anthologies. She was a prize winner in the 1989 World Haiku Contest and has twice received honorable mention for the Anna Davidson Rosenberg Award (1987, 1989), and in 1986 received first prize in the Hans S. Bodenheimer Poetry Award. She is the editor of *Her Soul Beneath the Bone: Women's Poetry on Breast Cancer* (University of Illinois Press, 1988) and of *Only Morning in her Shoes: Poetry about Old Women* (Utah State University Press, 1990).

Joan Lipkin

Joan Lipkin is the Artistic Director of That Uppity Theatre Company in St. Louis, Missouri where she founded the Alternate Currents/Direct Currents Series and The DisAbility Project. A playwright, fiction and screenwriter, director, teacher, and social activist, her award-winning work has been published and presented throughout the United States, Canada, Great Britain and Australia. She is published in numerous anthologies including *Amazon All Stars* (Applause), *Mythic Women/Real Women* (Faber & Faber), *Upstaging Big Daddy* (University of Michigan). "Silent Night" was previously published in *Nice Jewish Girls: Growing Up in America*, edited by Marlene Adler Marks in 1996, Plume/Penguin Books. It has been adapted into a short film, directed by Kathy Corley. Joan divides her time between St. Louis and other parts of the country

Cecile Low

Cecile Low, Born in Germany and raised in Belgium, spent the war years first in Belgium, in hiding, and then in Swiss internment camps. She came to America in 1954. In Belgium she was a teacher, in New York a secretary. Currently she is retired. She is a multilinguist, poet, freelance writer, member of Mensa, and President Emeritus of the New York Esperanto Society.

Janet Marks

Janet Marks has taught college English and Writing in Augusta, Georgia, Houston, and San Francisco, and ESL for several California Community Colleges. As runner-up for the Frances Shaw Fellowship for older women Writers, she was in residence at Ragdale, Lake Forest, Illinois for the month of July 1994. In 1992 and 1993, she won the Senior Award and Commendation Award for poems on the Jewish experience, sponsored by the Judah Magnes Museum.

Some of her poems have appeared in *New England Review, Mississippi Review, Forum, South and West, Songs for Our Voices*, Judah Magnes Museum, Berkeley, and *Poets on Parnassus Anthology*, San Francisco. She recently had poems in *Maelstrom* and *Curbside Review, Houston Poetry*

Fest Anthology '97 and *'98*, and has a poem coming out soon in *Mediphors*. She will appear in *Who's Who in America, 2001*.

Ruth Marmorstein

Ruth Marmorstein has often been told she is obsessed with the Holocaust. A full time writer, it appears in one form or another in most of her work. Married for forty-seven years to a survivor of Auschwitz and Buchenwald, she could only imagine what her husband, a boy of fifteen when taken from the ghetto, had endured while in camp and what he was like when liberated. In trying to understand and help her husband she read everything she could lay her hands on and then imparted her knowledge by lecturing. She spoke before groups trying to ignite a spark of interest in the subject long before anyone cared. She has transferred the passion of never forgetting the Holocaust to her four children.

Seymour Mayne

Seymour Mayne is the author, editor or translator of more than forty books and monographs. His most recent collections *include The Song of Moses and Other Poems* (Concertina/Menard Press, 1995), *City of the Hidden* [in Hebrew translation] (Gevanim, 1998), *Carbon Filter* (Mosaic Press, 1999), and a selection of humourous and satirical poems entitled *Light Industry* (Mosaic Press, 2000). He has also co-edited the award-winning anthologies, *Jerusalem: A Jewish Canadian Anthology* (Véhicule Press, 1996) and *A Rich Garland: Poems for A.M. Klein* (Véhicule Press, 1999), and translated a volume of Abraham Sutzkever's work from the Yiddish, *Burnt Pearls: Ghetto Poems* (Mosaic Press, 1981). He is a professor in the Department of English at the University of Ottawa.

Odette Meyers

Odette Meyers was born in Paris in November 1934. During WWII, her father was a prisoner of war in Germany, her mother was active in the Resistance, and their concierge "Madame Marie" protected them. After the Vel d'Hiv round up of July 16, 1942, Odette was sent to live in a Catholic family in Vendee. After eight months, her mother joined her to live under false identity in another village. All three survived. Other relatives died in camps. The family moved to Southern California in 1949. Married to the poet Bert Meyers with whom she had two children and from whom she was widowed in 1979, she taught French and French literature at the Claremont Colleges and in other college settings. Moving to Berkeley in 1980, she worked as a union then a community organizer in the San Francisco Bay Area. She became a survivor community advocate and activist, helping found survivor groups and help programs, participating in conferences on the Holocaust, writing articles and speaking in public. She appears in the film "The Courage to Care: Rescuers of Jews During the Holocaust" and her book of memoirs, *Doors to Madame Marie* was published by the University of Washington Press.

Rochelle Natt

The Holocaust is central to Rochelle Natt's life. She was named for a second cousin who was murdered by the Nazis in France. Her mother-in-law, Relly, and her parents and brothers had to leave all their possessions behind in Vienna when they made their narrow escape. Her father-in-law, Walter, went to a high school in Germany where no one would speak to him because he was Jewish. He managed to get out just in time, but his youngest brother was caught and sent to Auschwitz. One of her major themes as a writer is the undercurrent of dark memories in the children of survivors.

She has reviewed poetry for *American Book Review*, *ACM*, and *Kalliope*. She has published poetry in *Iowa Review, California Quarterly, Negative Capability, The Mac Giffin, Fresh Ground, Mudfish, Chachalaca Poetry Review, Astarte,* and in many anthologies.

Gary Pacernick

Since the publication of his Jewish poems as a book and their production as a play on stage and on Public Television, Gary Pacernick has continued to write about the Jewish experience. His most recent works in this vein are *Summer Psalms*, a limited edition with lithographs by the British artist Harvey Daniels and a collection of Dream Parables. He has published several critical studies on American Jewish poetry; edited the letters of the poet David Ignatow and edited the poetry magazine *Images*. Pacernick's *Meaning and Memory: Interviews with 14 Jewish Poets* is forthcoming from Ohio State University Press

Hedemarie Pilc

Hedemarie Pilc was born December 8, 1940 in the war-torn city of Ludwigshafen. She grew up in post-war Germany where she received a thorough education in language arts and literature. She worked as a reporter for music magazines and daily newspapers in Europe. In her twenties she got involved in the Jewish cause and studied the history of the Resistance movement against the Nazi Regime. In the late '70s she emigrated to California and succeeded in becoming an integral part of the West Coast jazz scene. In the early '90s she discovered her love of writing poetry and short stories. Her work has been published in anthologies and magazines and she has won prizes from Bay Area literary groups. She works as a freelance writer and is married to architect, Robert Pilc. They looking forward to becoming grandparents as their daughter, Esther Park, is expecting her first child.

Evelyn Posamentier

Evelyn Posamentier has written several books of poetry, and her work has been published in various magazines including the *American Poetry Review*. Her parents were from Vienna and fled to England in 1939; they arrived in New York City in 1940. Her four grandparents were killed in concentration camps. This publication of her poems is dedicated to the memory of her parents, Ernest and Alice Posamentier, and her grandparents, Otto and Gisela Epstein Pisk and Heinrich and Ernestine Schick Posamentier.

Dahlia Ravikovitch

Dahlia Ravikovitch was born in 1936 in Ramat Gan, a suburb of Tel Aviv. She studied at the Hebrew University in Jerusalem, and later worked as a journalist and teacher. Among her books are five volumes of poetry, *The Love of an Orange, A Hard Winter*, the third book, *Deep Unto Deep, True Love*, and *Mother and Child*; a book of short stories, *A Death in the Family*; and two books of poetry for children. She is the recipient of many of Israel's literary awards, including the Shlonsky, Brenner, Ussishkin and Bialik Prizes.

Barbara Reisner

Barbara Reisner lives in Allentown, Pennsylvania. Her work has appeared in *Manhattan Poetry Review, Bellingham Review, Wind Literary Journal, Creeping Bent, River Styx, Laurel Review, Yarrow, Blue Buildings, Stone Country, Poets On: Massachusetts Review, Graham House Review, Two Rivers Review, Shirim* and others. She has a chapbook published by Creeping Bent Press. Her poem, "Warsaw, 1946" was selected by the Peconic Gallery, Suffolk Community College, as part of their interdisciplinary exhibition on the subject of heroes in 1992.

Liliane Richman

Liliane Richman, born in Paris, France in 1940 and was hidden in the Southwest of France during the war with her brother Fred. Her father was a prisoner of war for five years, her mother was deported to Bergen-Belsen and returned in late 1945. She earned an M.A. in French and English and a Ph.D. degree in Philosophy/History of Ideas from the University of Texas in 1985. She has taught creative writing and French at Booker T. Washington H.S.P.V.A. in Dallas, Texas, since 1976.

She has published poetry and prose in several anthologies including *Two Worlds Walking* (New Rivers Press, 1995), *Blood to Remember* (Texas Tech University Press, 1993) *Movieworks* (Little Theater Press), *Song for Our Voices*, (Judah Magnes Museum, 1993) and *New Texas 93* (North Texas State U.). She has published in many journals and magazines including *Elf Magazine, Poets On:, Aileron, Nostalgia*, among others. Her poem won the 1998 Anna Davidson Rosenberg Award and she was first place winner in the National Poetry Competition of the 1997 Hackney Literary Awards, as well as the 1998 Borders' Poetry Competition in Dallas, Texas.

Shula Robin

Shula Robin was born in Poland in 1920. She left home before the war to study in Jerusalem and considers herself as one of the mothers of Israel. She arrived in Canada in 1957 and has lived in Toronto since 1970. Shula is the author of four poetry books: *Sunshine from Within, I Know Who I Am, I Begin to Understand* and *Mixed Blessings*. Her work has been set to music and performed in concert and last November a short video film based on her poem "At the Exhibition" was presented on an arts channel on TV. She has been interviewed on CBC Radio Canada and she continues to perform with a musician at museums, book fairs and other venues. Her short stories can be found on the Internet CBC Canadian Short Story Engine. Her prose book, *Journey on the River of Time*, is in search of a publisher.

Elizabeth Rosner

Elizabeth Rosner is a poet and novelist living in Berkeley, California. Her father is a survivor of Buchenwald concentration camp, and her mother survived the war by hiding in the Polish countryside. Rosner's prize-winning poetry and short fiction have appeared in numerous literary magazines, and her chapbook, *gravity*, was chosen for the Select Poets Series by Small Poetry Press. In 1995 she was named New/Emerging Poet by Alicia Ostriker in the Anna Davidson Rosenberg Contest for Poems on the Jewish Experience. Her first novel, *The Speed of Light*, which focuses on the effects of the Holocaust on the descendants of survivors, is to be published by Ballantine Books in the fall of 2001.

Bonnie Salomon

Dr. Salomon's parents, Helen and Simon, are Holocaust survivors. Born and raised in Poland, they survived Majdanek and Buchenwald, respectively. They emigrated to the United States in 1949. Bonnie Salomon is a physician in the Chicago area. "Munich. May, 1987" is an excerpt from a diary kept during a European tour after medical school. Dr. Salomon's essays and poems have appeared in *The Chicago Tribune* as well as many medical journals. A graduate of Harvard University, she trained in emergency medicine at Northwestern University. She recently completed a fellowship in clinical medical ethics at The University of Chicago. She lives with her husband, Michael and son Jonathan in Deerfield, Illinois.

Vera Schwartz

Vera Schwartz has been writing poetry since childhood and her work has appeared in local publications. Her particular subjects of interest are family relationships and matters pertaining to the Jewish experience. She is married with two grown children and two grandchildren of college age. Her parents were Russian immigrants who respected literature and encouraged their children to be creative in that area.

Myra Sklarew

Myra Sklarew was educated at Tufts University (biology) and Johns Hopkins (writing seminars); had coursework in bacterial genetics and viruses at Cold Spring Harbor Laboratory and coursework in immunology at NIH. She has been a member of the faculty, American University, Department of Literature since 1970 and co-director of the MFA Program in Creative Writing since 1980 with four and one-half years out as president of the Corporation of Yaddo, an artists' community. Early years included work as a research assistant, Yale University School of Medicine, Department of Neurophysiology.

Books published include: *From the Backyard of the Diaspora* (poetry), *The Science of Goodbyes* (poetry), *Altamira* (poetry), *Like a Field Riddled by Ants* (fiction), *Eating the White Earth* (poetry tr. Hebrew, published in Israel), *Lithuania: New & Selected Poems*. Forthcoming books: *Holocaust and the Construction of Memory* (nonfiction), *The Witness Trees* (poetry and essays), *From Mole Hills to Messiah* (essays).

Elizabeth Anne Socolow

Elizabeth Socolow is a poet who lives in Princeton, New Jersey with two cats. She teaches at the high school level and has taught since 1967 at colleges and universities in the East and the Midwest, including Vassar, Yale, Barnard, University of Michigan-Dearborn, Wayne State and Lawrence Technological Institute. She has two grown sons, one in London, England, the other in Washington, DC. In 1988, she won the Barnard Poetry Prize for her book *Laughing at Gravity: Conversations with Isaac Newton* (Beacon, 1988, out of print).

Jason Sommer

Jason Sommer is author of two collections of poetry: *Lifting the Stone* (Forest Books, London, 1991), and *Other People's Troubles* (University of Chicago Press, 1997), which won the Society of Midland Authors Poetry Award and was also a finalist for PEN U.S.A. West's literary prize for poetry. Sommer, a former Mirielees Fellow in Poetry at

Stanford University, has been Alan Collins Fellow in Poetry at Bread Loaf Writer's Conference, Walter E. Dakin Fellow in Poetry at Sewanee Writers' Conference, and has held a National Writers' Voice Project Community Residency. Sommer has received an Anna Davidson Rosenberg Award for poems about the Jewish experience and read his work at National Holocaust Memorial Museum. His poems have been widely anthologized, most recently in *The New American Poets*, (New England University Press in April 2000). He teaches literature and creative writing at Fontbonne College in St. Louis, Missouri.

Hans Jorg Stahlschmidt

Hans Jorg Stahlschmidt is a German writer and psychologist who moved to California eighteen years ago. He lives in Berkeley with his Jewish-American wife and their children. He has been involved in exploring the complexity of the German-Jewish relationship for many years. His poetry has appeared in many journals and anthologies, among them *Madison Review*, *Atlanta Review*, *Manoa*, *Texas Poetry Review*, and *Anthology of Magazine Verse* and *Yearbook of American Poetry*. He has received several prizes in national and international poetry competitions.

Elaine Starkman

Elaine Starkman is co-editor of the award winning collection *HERE I AM: Contemporary Jewish Stories from Around the World*, (JPS, 1998) and author of *Learning to Sit in the Silence: A Journal of Caretaking*, 1993. She lives and teaches in Northern California. She will have her first stories published online at write-on-line.co.uk.

Hannah Stein

Hannah Stein lives and writes in Davis, California. She teaches poetry workshops at the Davis Art Center and is currently finishing a five-year tour of duty as editor of the political/literary magazine *Americas Review*. Her full-length collection, *Earthlight*, is the first volume in the La Questa Press Poetry series. State Street Press published her chapbook, *Schools of Flying Fish*. Her poetry has appeared in *The Antioch Review*, *The Yale Review*, *Beloit Poetry Journal*, *Poetry Flash*, *Poetry Northwest*, *Prairie Schooner*, *Calyx*, *ForPoetry.com* and *Webdelsol's Perihelion*.

Stein has won national awards and has been nominated for a Pushcart Prize. "Twin", the poem which appears in this volume, was the first-prize winner in the Judah P. Magnes Museum's first Anna Davidson Rosenberg contest for poetry on the Jewish experience. Her father was one of three of the family's six children who emigrated to America before Hitler. The rest of the family perished in the Holocaust.

Susan Terris

Susan Terris' book *Curved Space*, was published in 1998 (La Jolla Poets Press). In 1999, she had two books published: *Eye of the Holocaust*, (Arctos Press) and *Angels of Bataan* (Pudding House Publications). Other recent books include *Killing in the Comfort Zone* (Pudding House Publications) and *Nell's Quilt* (Farrar, Straus & Giroux). Her journal publications include *The Antioch Review, The Midwest Quarterly, Missouri Review, Nimrod, Southern California Anthology,* and *The Southern Poetry Review*. In 1998-2000, Ms. Terris was nominated for two Pushcart Prizes. She also won the first place in six poetry competitions, and was a second place winner or finalist in sixteen national competitions.

Barbara Unger

Barbara Unger is the co-author, with Lloyd Ultan, of *Bronx Accent: a Literary and Pictorial History of the Borough*, (Rutgers University Press, 2000), which won an award from the J. M. Kaplan Fund. Barbara spent the first thirty years of her life in The Bronx, New York. Only within the last year, while tracing her family roots through the Internet, did she learn about the death of some of her mother's family members at Babi Yar. She has published five books of poetry and a collection of short fiction. Among her publications are; *Basement* (Isthmus Press, 1975): *The Man who Burned Money* (the Bellevue Press, 1980): *Blue Depression Glass* (Thorntree Press, 1991) and *Dying For Uncle Ray and Other Stories* (Kendall/Hunt, 1990). She is a Professor of English at Rockland Community College of The State University of New York. Unger's work has won awards from NYSCA, The National Endowment for the Humanities and the National Endowment for the Arts, and the Anna Davidson Rosenberg Award from the Judah Magnes Museum, among others.

Henny Wenkart

Born in Vienna, Henny Wenkart arrived in this country aboard S.S. President Harding on a children's transport June 3, 1939. Most of her family joined her just as war broke out in Europe. She attended Pembroke College, got her masters degree at Radcliffe and received a Ph.D. in 1970 from Harvard. While working on the Ph.D., Henny originated a set of children's readers, *Teaching Jonny's Sister to Read*, and built them into a home-based small press, selling 300,000 copies between 1963 and 1970. In New York, she taught at Stern College for Women. She originated and edited *Sarah's Daughters Sing*, an anthology (KTAV 1990), and most recently she originated and co-edited the anthology, *Which Lilith?* (Jason Aronson, 1998) and completed the translations of *Memoirs of a Grandmother*, by the nineteenth-century writer Pauline Wengeroff (University Press of Maryland, 2000). Her poems have appeared in fine literary journals including *Prairie Schooner, Confrontation, Paterson Literary Review*, and others, and in a number of anthologies. She is at work on a novel, *No Harm*, and on a philosophical book on George Santayana, as well as further volumes of the Jewish Women's Literary annual. Her book of poems is titled *Philanderer's Wife*.

Ruth Whitman

Ruth Whiman is a widely published poet, author and translator. She has published several collections of poetry and two books on poetic method. Her translations include *The Selected Poems of Jacob Glatstein* and *An Anthology of Modern Yiddish Poetry*. Whitman was lecturer in poetry for Radcliffe Seminars of Radcliffe College. She held an M.A. from Harvard University. Sadly, Ms. Whitman passed away on December 1, 1999.

Juliet Zarembski

Juliet Zarembski was born in Princeton, New Jersey and graduated from New York University with both B.A. and M.A. degrees in English Literature. Juliet has received numerous awards for her poetry and scholarship including the Anna Davidson Rosenberg Award for Poetry and the 1996 Dean's Award for Scholarship and Service from

New York University. She was a national finalist in the British Marshall Scholarship as a result of her extensive research on Sylvia Plath. The author of poems, fiction and editorial features, Juliet has spent most of her professional career as an editor and public relations executive. She is married and lives in New Jersey.

Laura Zusman

Laura Zusman is currently a student at the University of Michigan, Ann Arbor. She wrote "My Weeping Willow" at the age of twelve for a Holocaust memorial service at her synagogue. It was selected for this volume because it was considered exquisitely sensitive, mature and compassionate for a child of that age. Recently she returned from her first journey to Israel, where she was touched by a visit to the Holocaust memorial, Yad Vashem. Writing continues to be one of her favorite pastimes, as well as singing, dancing, and playing the flute.